CONTENTS

HOW TO TRAIN A PUPPY

MASTER DOG TRAINING

How to TRAIN
== A ==
PUPPY

A Beginner's Guide to Raising a Puppy
with Positive Training

Kenneth Binmoeller

INTRODUCTION

Congratulations on purchasing *How to Train a Puppy* and thank you for doing so.

So, you have decided that you want to raise a puppy. Congratulations! This is a major change in your life that should not be taken lightly. If you are ready to add a puppy to your family, you are committing to taking care of another living creature for the duration of its natural life. You are committing to meeting not only the puppy's physical needs for food, water, and shelter but also socializing your puppy, ensuring that your puppy remains stimulated regularly, and overall making sure the puppy is kept happy.

This can be quite demanding in many ways—puppies, especially when they are young, can require around the clock care and potty breaks, much like how you would have to wake up constantly to take care of a baby. Puppies will not be able to talk to you to tell you what is wrong, and they will always require some degree of care throughout the day just due to the fact that they are not self-sufficient. They cannot let themselves outside unless you happen to have a doggy door. They cannot put food into their own bowls or get themselves water. You will be responsible for another living being's round-the-clock needs.

If that is intimidating to you, you may want to consider some other sort of pet. You may find that you are not actually a dog person, and that is okay. It takes real grace to admit that, and it is better that you take more time to consider just a large decision rather than attempting to force something that will not work out. If it will not work out, that is okay.

Within this book, you will be introduced to everything that you need to know about taking care of a puppy. You will learn what to expect with training a puppy, how the mind of your puppy will work, and why you should make sure that your puppy is a well-trained dog to begin with. You will learn what not to do with your puppy, as well as how to take care of its basic needs. You will be guided through how to teach your puppy everything that he or she needs to know, how to housebreak your puppy, and how to choose which commands your puppy should learn. You will be given several tricks and tips to training your puppy, as well as how to correct some of the most common behavioral problems that you are likely to encounter.

At the end of the day, however, it will be up to you to figure out how to approach this process. You will have to decide what it is that your puppy wants or needs and how to ensure that those needs are met. You will have to determine whether a puppy fits into your lifestyle or if you are setting yourself up for failure in trying to bring them into your life to begin with. Hopefully, by the time you have finished reading this book, you will know whether you have made the right and responsible decision to bring a dog into your life in the first place.

TRAINING A PUPPY: EVERYTHING YOU NEED TO KNOW

PUPPIES, like people, learn in stages. They develop over time, much like people do. They require constant supervision in the early days and behave much like a destructive toddler. If you think you can leave your puppy alone unsupervised while you go to work all day, think again—just as you cannot leave a toddler alone unsupervised for an extended period of time, you cannot leave your puppy home alone either.

*H*owever, unlike a child, a puppy can be trained much quicker. Thanks to the fact that puppies reach maturity far sooner than people do, the periods of time in which your puppy is entirely and utterly reliant on you to keep him or her from destroying things is much lower, so long as you put the work in. You must be willing and able to train your pup in order to ensure that he or she will be able to understand his or her place and role in the house and in your family. To some degree, this will involve understanding dominance and your dog—recognizing how it becomes critically important for you to make sure that all humans rank higher in the hierarchy than the dog does. However, that does not mean that you need to be aggressive—we will be going over the difference between assertiveness and aggressiveness later within this book.

*W*ithin this chapter, we are going to address what training a puppy will generally look like. We will go over how a dog sees the world so you will be able to ensure that your own training is successful in the first place. We will go over the benefits of having a well-trained dog, and go over the importance of choosing a breed that fits the lifestyle that you live. No two breeds of dogs are identical, and the sooner you recognize this, the sooner you will be able to make those important changes that you would like to see.

*T*raining Puppies

Training puppies is not necessarily a difficult thing to do —but it is something that can become quite tedious if you are not particularly engaged in the process. It is absolutely hard work—but it is absolutely critical to your puppy's development. Ultimately, your puppy will rely on you to make him or her the perfect canine citizen. He or she will be dependent upon you to sculpt his or her behavior into that of a well-behaved dog. Ultimately, this world is quite intolerant of dogs that are not well-behaved. They are expected to be trained well firstly due to a safety issue if a dog is not properly trained and socialized, but secondly due to assuming that your dog will have good manners when you do take it out and about.

· · ·

*W*hen you are going to be training your puppy, you are looking to do so in very short periods at any given point in time. You are going to be wanting to incorporate training as soon as you get your pup. You may be using simple obedience training, for example, to encourage and facilitate your dog in becoming accustomed to listening to you. You may be teaching simple commands such as sit or stay. Ultimately, you are going to want to do this training several times throughout the day for roughly 5 minutes at a time. They do not have very long attention spans, especially in those early days, and you want to make sure that you are regularly encouraging and facilitating that training through repetition. This will help you to reinforce the training as it is happening.

*W*hen you are training, the key is ensuring that it is something positive. It should be positive and happy, with you doing your best to focus on positive reinforcement as it happens. This will not only help strengthen the bond between you and your puppy, it will also allow for your puppy to learn better sooner.

The Inner Workings of the Dog's Mind

It may come as a shock to you, but a dog does, in fact, think. Dogs, once they are fully grown, usually have the same level of cognition that you would expect to see in a child between the ages of 3 and 5. They are capable of recognizing what you are pointing at. They can tell which bowl of food or water has more than another. They can tell what is going on with body language. They will naturally pick up on how to communicate with you in ways that you can recognize and understand yourself.

*H*owever, even with that sort of cognition capability, you will find that your dog cannot be reasoned with in the way that you would reason with a 3-year-old child. You cannot tell your dog not to climb onto the furniture because you do not like the fur that is all over it. What you can do, however, is work on how to teach your dog to follow through with what you want. You will want to find that dogs and puppies are quite capable of learning about the world around them, but that learning will happen somewhat differently.

*Y*ou will want to be focusing on either giving your dog positive attention or not at all to get the point across with your dog's behavior. This means that telling your dog no and scolding it is not likely to be effective, but what you can do is ignore your dog entirely when they are doing something that they should not be doing. This is because your dog wants to please you. Dogs are literally bred to please us—they developed and evolved alongside humans to become reliant on us and therefore, they look to us on a regular basis. You will be able to keep this in mind when you are training your dog. Remember that you are asserting yourself as the calm, in-charge leader. Your dog will need gentle but firm redirection and training from you. Your dog will feel more secure when you are able to be firm and clear with boundaries and with expectations, especially when they are consistent. All of this must be remembered if you want to hope to train your pup into a well-behaved canine citizen.

The Benefits of Having a Well-Trained Dog

When you train your puppy, you are creating all sorts of benefits, both for yourself and for your dog. You are ensuring that you are meeting your dog's need to be able to fit in—you are ensuring that your dog is able to become a well-behaved member of your family by ensuring that your dog knows how to meet your expectations. When you train your dog to be obedient, you ensure that your dog is going to look to you—you will be in complete control of your dog. This is powerful because it allows you to establish yourself as the leader that your dog will be looking up to. When you do this, you ensure that your dog is going to be looking to you regularly. You ensure that your dog is entirely interested in your own interpretations of the world around it and that your dog wants to please you. This is important for all sorts of reasons, such as:

- **Safety:** A dog that you cannot control can do a lot of damage. People can, and regularly do, die from dog attacks, and many of these deaths can actually be prevented if the dogs are taken care of and trained properly. Of course, your dog is a living, breathing creature that is capable of acting unpredictably, but most of the time, when you have a dog that you have trained well, they will listen to you, even if they do not necessarily want to at that point in time. You will be able to recall your dog to get them back to your side. You will be able to ensure that they do not snarl over their food bowl when your toddler inevitably tries to reach into it while your dog is eating. You will make sure that your dog will not jump up on people and hurt them. Especially if you have a dog that is larger, you are going to want to ensure that it is well trained for everyone's safety —your dog's included.
- **Control:** A dog that you cannot control is a dog that is a risk to other people. Your dog may run away if you cannot control him. Your dog may try to attack a cat if you cannot

recall him. Your dog may harass other people or bark incessantly if you cannot command him to be quiet. Some of these may be simple annoyances, but others can pose real safety risks as well. You need to be able to control your dog to ensure that your dog does not impact other people.

- **Bonding:** When you are working on training your puppy, you are facilitating a strong bond built on trust. You are teaching your dog that you are someone that can be looked up to and trusted, and that will make your dog calmer and more confident. Dogs thrive in settings where there are strict rules and expectations. When you can ensure that your dog is likely to follow those rules and expectations, you can make sure that your dog bonds to you better.

- **Easier time taking your dog out:** When you have a dog, you may decide that you want to take him or her out places. Whether it is to the park, the dog park, or on a trip and into a hotel for the weekend, you need a dog that is well behaved. When you ensure that your dog is, in fact, well trained, you will be able to do this with ease because your dog will have better manners.

- **Better socialization skills:** When you train your dog the right way, you ensure that he or she learns all of those important social skills in life that will allow your dog to go out and spend time with other dogs. When a dog is not well trained, it can end up pestering other dogs or acting in ways that other dogs deem inappropriate, making it difficult, or even impossible in some situations, to create those interactive settings between your dog and others.

Choosing a Breed That Is Right for You

As one final point to consider within this chapter, you must learn how to identify what kind of dog is right for you to begin with. This will be incredibly important for you—you need to ensure that the dog that you choose is one that will fit in with your lifestyle just due to the fact that there are so many different breeds of dogs out there. In fact, there are right around 200 dog breeds out there that are currently recognized by the AKC, and then you have to consider all of the mixed breeds and mutts that exist as well. This means that you have many different options out there for you to decide between.

When you are trying to choose a dog for your own family, there are many different considerations that you will need to make to ensure that ultimately, the dog that you have chosen is one that will fit neatly into your own current lifestyle. Let's go over a few of the different considerations that you need to make.

Your Experience With Dogs

Some dogs are naturally more obedient than others. Some dogs, such as Huskies and Shiba Inus are dogs that will require far more effort and experience than a dog that naturally wants to please you. If you are reading this book, there is a very good chance that you are a beginner to owning a puppy on your own, and because of that, you should aim for a breed that is usually going to be deemed easygoing or easy to train.

. . .

Your Space Available to You

Just because you are in a city apartment without a yard does not mean that you cannot get a dog. In fact, many different breeds of dogs can actually do great inside without a yard, so long as you are willing and able to take them out to run around on a regular basis. Consider breeds that are going to be better suited to apartment life when you are doing your research if you live in one. If you have a yard, consider how big and how secure it is as well.

Your Current Family Dynamic

Another point to consider when trying to choose your dog will be whether or not you have children and whether those children are younger and therefore more likely to annoy your dog at some point or another. Some dogs do great with children—for example, golden retrievers are often considered the quintessential family dog due to their patience with children. Other dogs, however, such as Chihuahuas, may get nippy with children that they perceive as a threat.

How Much Noise You Can Tolerate

Dogs can vary greatly in terms of how vocal they will become and you will have to decide just how much noise you are willing and able to accept from them. You must decide if constant barking and whining is going to be a problem for you or if you want a dog that is largely quiet and will only bark when needed. This is going to be up to personal preference. While you may be able to influence just how loud or quiet your dog may be, you will find that some breeds are generally much yappier than others.

How Much Maintenance Is Required

You may need to also consider if you want a dog that will require meticulous grooming or one that is going to be more clean than not. Some dogs will shed more than others. Some dogs will require regular bathing and haircuts. Some dogs will drool all over the place, and other dogs will be relatively low maintenance. You must know exactly how much you are willing to put up with so you can make an informed decision.

How Big of a Dog You Want

You will also need to be well aware of how large of a dog that you want, or if you live in a rental unit, how large of a dog you can have. Many rental units have rules in place that limit the size of dogs within their apartments and you will need to consider this yourself. You will also need to consider that larger dogs will usually eat more and may also require more space and exercise than smaller dogs, though that is not always the case. Larger dogs may also be more difficult to control when unruly than smaller ones—for example, you may be able to lift up a Chihuahua that is harassing someone, but if your lab goes running after someone and you are a relatively small person, you may find that you are yanked along without any real recourse.

How Active You Are or Are Willing to Be

Finally, as one last point to consider, you may want to

look at dogs that have a similar exercise and activity level to what you already have going on in your life. If you are a couch potato, you are not going to want to adopt a big working dog under the assumption that getting said big working dog will help you feel motivated to get off the couch and go work out. You do not know if that is the case—you may get lazy about it, or you may decide that it is not worth the effort and then you have a dog that you are not taking care of properly. Some dogs will be perfectly happy being couch potatoes along with you, so long as you give them a quick 10- minute walk, but others will insist on much more exercise, with some of the working breeds needing at least an hour or two of vigorous exercise throughout the day.

WHAT NOT TO DO

As we begin to move along, it becomes important to begin looking at some of the most common puppy training mistakes that get made on a regular basis. Consider this your guide on exactly what NOT to do when you get your puppy and first bring him or her home. They will only make life more difficult for you and can actually seriously hinder your attempts to train your puppy at all. Let's take a look at some of the most common mistakes now.

You Use the Command, "No, [Puppy's Name]"

This is a major mistake for one particular reason: When you are constantly pairing, "no," with your puppy's name, you are teaching your dog that they should associate their name with the word, "No." This is a problem—you have suddenly taught your pup that his name is something to be afraid of or something to be avoided or stopped. Instead of your dog being happy to see you or hear you call his name, your dog will instead be hesitant—he will hear his name and freeze up, assuming that he has done something wrong to begin with, and that will seriously hurt you and your pup's relationship later down the line.

*Y*ou Use the Command, "No," At All

Similarly, you may find that you eliminate this command altogether. No is an incredibly nonspecific command. While we understand the nuances behind the word and we understand that it means that you are telling the dog not to do that one activity that they are just doing that moment, your dog does not get the message. Remember, your dog does not speak English—to your dog, telling him no could sometimes mean to get down, but other times mean to be quiet. Sometimes, the command is used to get the dog to stop barking, but other times the command is used to tell him to stop running. It is incredibly confusing for a dog that does not understand what it is that you are asking him or her to do in the first place and because of that, you should try to eliminate this command from your vocabulary.

*I*nstead, try teaching your dog other commands that can be used. If you are trying to tell your dog that they cannot jump on the couch with you, you could try telling your dog, "Down," instead. That is a very specific command that always has the same exact result: Your dog puts all feet on the floor. When you use a very specific command with your pup instead of trying to teach them nonspecific words, you will find that they better understand what your expectation is and because of that, they are better able to meet those expectations in the first place.

. . .

*Y*ou Don't Start Training Immediately

Dog training should start almost immediately upon arriving home. It used to be believed that you should not start it until somewhere between 6 months and a year, but nowadays, it is known that waiting that year is a good way to solidify all sorts of bad behaviors that you would otherwise like to avoid. Instead of allowing your puppy to run rampant until he or she is older, recognize that you can start training on day 1. You can teach your pup to recognize and respect boundaries early on, and starting immediately gives your pup a head start over his or her peers. When you are already actively attempting to train your pup on how to behave, you know that your pup is going to be that much more likely to follow behaviors later on because you have already set that foundation for yourself.

*Y*ou Don't Want to Be Inconsistent With Commands

Some people may find it hard to resist repeating their commands over and over again. They may be trying to get their dog to stay, for example, by saying, "Stay. Stay. Stay. Stay. Stay." However, there is a problem with this—when you are repeating yourself over and over again, you are teaching your dog that they need to follow your commands, but only after you have repeated that command several times over, and that is a problem. When you do this with your dog, you will teach him or her that the command is not simply, "Stay." But rather, repeating the world five times over, and they will not actively stay until you do exactly that —tell them to stay five times in a row.

. . .

*Y*ou Punish Your Puppy When You Discover the Problem

Oftentimes, people do not realize that their puppy has done something undesirable until after the fact. Perhaps you found that your favorite shoe has been chewed up earlier in the day, so you go stomping over to your pup, shove your chewed-up shoe in the pup's face and start to scold him. However, there is a problem with this—dogs think in the moment. They do not really understand what it is that they did earlier, nor do they realize or understand that you are currently scolding behavior that happened earlier. They think that you are scolding what they are doing in that particular moment rather than what they did earlier and you are missing the lesson.

*T*his goes double for potty training—if you find that your pup has had an accident, you cannot walk your pup over to said accident and attempt to scold him or her. You cannot make it clear to your pup that you are angry about the accident in any way—not even by rubbing his or her nose in it, which is something that you should never, ever do under any circumstance.

*Y*ou Use Physical Discipline

Some people think that since they cannot speak and reason with their dogs, the only way that they have to get their point across is with physical discipline in an attempt to get them to submit. However, this is not the case. All that happens when you attempt to dominate your dog through such methods is that you teach your dog not to trust you at all, damaging your relationship with him or her and making it harder for you to really bond.

Calling Your Dog to You for Discipline

Another mistake that all too many people make is calling their dog to them when they plan on doing something unpleasant. Whether you are going to be scolding your dog, calling them for bath time, or to get in the car to go to the vet, when you call your dog to you in order to do something that your dog will not enjoy, you run the risk of making them decide that they will avoid you. They will not want to come to you when they know that sometimes, going to you is not the pleasant thing that it should be. They will see it as something that is quite possibly unpleasant, so they avoid it whenever possible.

Treating Your Dog Like a Person

People will oftentimes personalize their dog. They will treat their dog like they would treat their children—and this is a problem. Firstly, your dog is not your child. Your dog is not a human. Your dog does not think like a human or have the wants of a human. Your dog is certainly deserving of the same respect that you would afford any other living being, but you should not be allowing your dog to do whatever he or she wants. When your dog looks at you like an equal rather than a leader, you are going to set your dog up to rebel when he or she wants. Your dog may feel like you are not the one in control of all of these different situations around him or her and because of that he will begin to take liberties that you would rather not afford. For this particular reason, it is important to remember that your dog is a dog and that is it.

THE CARE AND KEEPING OF YOUR PUPPY

WITH THOSE COMMON mistakes behind you, it is time to begin looking at some of the most important ways in which you will be caring for your puppy. We are going to be going over general guidelines for all of the general care and keeping of your dog. We are going to be addressing how to groom your puppy, how to pick out food for your puppy, how to exercise your puppy, how to play with your puppy, how often to take your puppy out to relieve him or herself, and how to train your puppy. Each of these is incredibly important aspects of puppy ownership and if you cannot recognize how to meet these needs with your own pup, you are going to find that you struggle.

Grooming Your Puppy

Grooming pups is something that should happen depending upon their coats. Some pups only need occasional baths while others may need more. As a general rule, your pup will need a bath or grooming once a month. You may decide to do this yourself, or you may find that you are better off paying for a groomer to take care of it.

*G*enerally speaking, when you take your dog to a groomer, your dog will get the whole treatment in one. They will be able to bathe your pup, as well as brush and dry them. They will be able to clean your dog's ears out to ensure that there is no earwax, and also make sure that any trimming of fur or hair is done. Beyond just that, there will be trimming done for your dog's toenails, and usually, the teeth will also be brushed.

*O*f course, you can choose to do all of this yourself at home, as well. You will just need to make sure that you have all of the tools to do so. You will want to look up a guide on your specific dog's breed to get more information about what will be required and how you can ensure that your pup's hygiene is always taken care of. Generally speaking, however, you will want to ensure that you have a good brush specific to your pup's fur type, which can vary greatly from breed to breed. You will need to have shampoo designed for use on dogs in particular, who may have much more sensitive skin than you do. You will want to ensure that you use guillotine-style clippers for your dog's nails and you will need to be careful not to clip the quick to avoid bleeding. Just in case, however, you will want to have styptic powder on hand in case you do happen to trim too short and hit the quick to cause bleeding. You may find, especially if you have a dog that sheds a lot, that it is easier just to take him or her to the groomer once a month than it is to deal with everything else yourself, and that is okay! No matter what, however, you will want to ensure that your pup is getting cleaned up regularly.

Feeding Your Puppy

Another important aspect of dog ownership is ensuring that your pup is getting the right nutrition at all times. This means that you will need to figure out exactly what it is that your pup needs to be fed and happy. This will largely vary from pup to pup and you are going to be best served looking up what kind of food and diet is going to be best for the breed that you have. Generally speaking, any of the food that you get at the pet store will be at the very least of a good enough quality to be fed to your pup—it will be edible. However, that is about as much as you can really determine. Some dog food is going to be better than others—some dog food is packed up full of grains and scraps that are not particularly nutritious for your pup. They may be full of fillers and some multivitamins that are meant to balance them out. Other dog foods will be made with meat instead of meat byproducts and they will generally be a bit healthier for your pup to be consuming. As a general rule, the more expensive the dog food that you get, the higher the quality generally is. This is not a hard and fast rule, however—what is going to matter more is that the food is going to be made of whole food products instead of byproducts or animal meal. When you can make sure that you are choosing the right sorts of food, you will be able to ensure that the food that your pup is getting is going to be healthier in general for him.

*O*f course, if you have the time to do so, the best choice for pups will almost always be having their dog food homemade. This will require you to figure out exactly what your particular dog's nutritional requirements will be, however, and you will want to ensure that you can do this by learning what you can online. You will then have to look into how to balance out that nutritional requirements with your own whole foods. This is a bit more time consuming at first, and it may be costlier than other options, but will probably be the healthiest for your dog. Over time, you will get the experience that you will need to simply make a batch of dog food once a week, or even once a month if you decide to freeze and store it, and you will know exactly what your pup is eating.

*A*s well as ensuring that your pup is fed, usually to a schedule, you will want to make sure that you always have water available for him or her to drink. Usually, your pup will take care to drink as needed so you will not have to worry too much about whether he or she is getting enough water. Nevertheless, you will want to keep an eye to make sure that he or she is, in fact, drinking at all. Some pups struggle to drink with deep bowls and you may need to try providing a shallower dish for them to drink from.

*E*xercising Your Puppy

Dogs of all kinds need exercise. They need this to keep them healthy and strong. The amount of exercise may vary greatly from dog to dog, but they will still need to get up and active at least for some period of time each day. Most dogs are not likely to exercise themselves even if you do allow them to go outside—you will need to be actively engaging with your dog and following your dog to ensure that he or she is actually doing what he is doing. Most dogs need somewhere between 30 minutes and 2 hours of exercise within a day, depending on the breed. Working dogs will generally require more, whereas smaller dogs will typically not require much at all.

. . .

*E*xercise can be facilitated in many different ways. You may, for example, exercise your dog with a leisurely walk through the neighborhood a few times a day. Other dogs, however, will have much more vigorous needs and may require you to actively hike or work them. Your pup, if you do not exercise him or her adequately is likely to fall into all sorts of negative or destructive behaviors, which is precisely the reason why you *do* need to be mindful of what you are doing with them and ensuring that they are being worked enough. When they are not worked enough, they will oftentimes find other ways to burn that energy that you would rather not deal with.

*P*laying with Your Puppy

Playing with your pup is another regular expectation that you need to meet. Your pup or dog will always want to spend time with you, and that time will be spent in all sorts of different ways. Your pup may want to play tug-o-war with you or play fetch with you. No matter how you chose to play with your dog, however, you are facilitating a better bond with them. You will be able to make your dog feel more bonded and attached to you when you are regularly sharing these sorts of positive interactions with each other and those positive interactions are what you are looking to see with them.

*O*f course, this playtime is also a great way for you to facilitate more exercise as well. It can be a way for you to kill two birds with one stone—you can play fetch at the dog part, for example, encouraging your pup to get up, on his feet, and running around. You can get your pup actively running and in doing so, you will find that he or she is going to be happier in general. Your pup will feel like that social need has been met and that is incredibly important.

*O*nce again, if you do not take the time to play with your dog to keep him or her socially and mentally stimulated, you are going to find that you wind up with a destructive dog. Your dog will not be very well behaved if he or she is bored. You ultimately want to wear your dog out. A tired dog is always going to be a good dog.

*T*aking Your Puppy Outside

You may be wondering now how often you need to worry about taking your pup out to use the bathroom. Generally speaking, a pup can hold their bladder for roughly as many hours as the age they are, plus one. This means that a two-month-old puppy should never be expected to hold it longer than three hours, and if you really want to be successful at training them, you are going to want them to go out even more regularly. You will want to aim for every hour or two for young puppies during the day, and then every 3 or so hours at night. Yes, this means that you are going to be waking up throughout the night for the first few months—if you are not prepared for this, you may decide that you will get a puppy that is older, or that you will adopt an adult dog, which is always an option as well.

*G*enerally speaking, you will want to take your pup outside right after eating or drinking, right after waking up, and right after he or she has been playing for a while. These are the most likely times that your pup is going to want to go to relieve him or herself, and you are going to want to take your pup out more often than he or she will need to avoid running into problems with accidents later on.

*Y*ou will also want to look for any signs that your pup needs to go out as well—you will usually see signs such as pacing, whining, or walking in circles. Some pups will also sniff at the ground to find a suitable spot. If you see any of this, assume that it is a potty emergency and get your pup out immediately. If you do happen to mistime things and end up with an accident, ensure that you clean it up promptly with enzyme cleaners that are designed to eliminate the scent of waste. If you do not entirely destroy the odor in that area, your pup will go back to that spot to go, over and over again.

*T*raining Your Puppy

Finally, the last major point of the day-to-day care of your pup is going to be ensuring that you are following through with your training of him or her. This is something that we are going to be looking at in-depth shortly—it involves ensuring that your pup is being taught what is expected on a regular basis. You will want to ensure that your training starts immediately, and once you do start to train your pup, you want to ensure that you remain consistent and reliable. You will want to make sure that you are constantly practicing those behaviors that you are attempting to facilitate and that you are ensuring that your pup is learning the commands that he or she needs. Just like with potty training, you will want to ensure that your training is being constantly reinforced. You may even start to begin a routine in which you work on obedience training for a few short minutes each and every time that your pup comes in from relieving him or herself. When you can do this on the regular, you will find that your pup is much more likely and willing to follow along with what you are suggesting. This is absolutely a need for your pup that must be met just as often as the needs for food and water.

TEACHING YOUR PUPPY

WHEN YOU ARE ready to train your puppy, there are a few key points to remember if you really want to be successful. These points will help you make sure that you are effective in how you interact with your puppy and be as firm and fair of a leader as you can to him or her. Ultimately, people are commonly making many of the mistakes that we have gone over thus far in the book. People will find that they repeatedly make these mistakes over and over again and as a result, they find that they wind up with a puppy that is poorly trained in some way. However, you can learn to mitigate that by remembering the five principles that you will be given in this chapter.

The Importance of Positivity

Positivity is almost always more effective at long-term training than negativity. Imagine, for example, that you want to train your pup to stay off of your couch. Now, your couch is comfortable. Your couch is also where you are sitting, and your pup is going to naturally want to be around you because he or she loves you. Let's say that your puppy decides to jump up on the couch. What do you do next?

*Y*ou can now choose whether you are going to respond negatively to this—you may yell at the pup, throw something at the pup, push the pup off of the couch, or all of the above. For the record, none of this is treatment that your pup should be enduring at all, but consider it for the point of this example. This is all negative training. You are making the stimulus of jumping onto the couch negative in hopes that your pup will learn not to do it at all. There are even products these days designed to do just that. However, your pup isn't learning to stay off of the couch—your pup is learning to stay off of the couch when you are around. He is afraid of your response and so he avoids it as much as he can when he knows you are around.

*W*hen you use positive training, however, you encourage your pup to recognize something—you are teaching your pup that you are happier when your pup is on the floor. You gently put the pup on the floor and pat his head and offer a treat and some praise. This tells your pup that good things happen when all feet are on the floor as opposed to bad things happening when he tries to climb up when you are around.

*P*ositive training then becomes much more motivational. Your pup learns to associate the training that you want with good things—praise, treats, and attention. All of those are great motivators for pups. They are entirely happy to receive it, which is precisely why you should consider doing things in this manner.

The Importance of Consistency

Beyond just remaining positive with your puppy, you must also ensure that you are always consistent. Dogs thrive on consistency. Consistency is predictable, regulates their expectations, and allows them to know exactly what they can and cannot do. When you are training your pup, that means that you must always use the same commands as everyone else that is currently training. Make sure that everyone is using the same words, the same methods, and the same rewards for the commands you are training.

You will also want to ensure that you get your puppy on some sort of a schedule that will aid you in ensuring that your pup learns to do what is needed with ease. You can do this by making it a routine to take your pup out at certain times, followed by a predictable schedule of training, feeding, playing, and napping. When you keep your pup on a consistent schedule, you know that you r pup is comfortable with what is happening around you. You and your pup will be able to act with each other in perfect sync when you learn how to line up those expectations and consistency.

The Line Between Firm and Harsh

Another important thing to consider is the difference between firm and being harsh. You can be quite firm without ever saying or doing anything mean. You can also be quite harsh without saying a mean word. When you are talking to your pup, you want to ensure that you are always firm with him or her. In remaining firm, you can assert that you are in control and that is important. You need to be able to remain in control so your pup knows that he or she can count on you. Your pup will naturally turn to you—his instincts tell him that you are in charge, especially when you do take back that control and power, and when you can work with that with ease, you will show your pup that he can trust you.

*H*owever, when you are too harsh with your pup, you run the risk of scaring him. You need to recognize that the difference between assertion and aggression is exceedingly slim, but it is one that matters greatly. Assertion and ensuring that your pup knows what you are expecting is one thing, but snapping at your pup and yelling at him for getting something wrong is an entirely different matter altogether.

*B*eing firm involves being calm. You must be calm in order to interact with your pup in a way that is not going to upset him. This is because your pup will pick up on your stress. Your pup will know when you are not happy and that stresses your pup out, too. Your pup wants to be able to know that you are happy—he wants to please you. However, he cannot do that if he does not know what he is doing or how he should. Assertion is calm and firm. Aggression is the result of anger mixing in with assertion. Keep this in mind and make sure that you always do your best to respond in a way that is calm.

The Right Tone

When you are training your pup, tone is everything. Firstly, your pup knows what a harsh tone is—it will immediately put your pup on the defensive and no good learning happens when that occurs. You need your pup to be able to understand you and be in a learning mood for you to be able to train him, but being harsh or angry is not going to do that.

When you are talking to your pup, you want to use higher-pitched tones. Dogs in general naturally tend to gravitate toward those tones. They respond well to whistles, for example, because the whistle cuts through everything else and allows the pup to focus on one thing in particular. This means that you should also speak to your pup in a tone that is higher as well. Not only are higher tones usually perceived as more positive and pleasant, your pup will be able to better make out your words.

Think about how people speak to toddlers—their voices go up an octave or so and they slow down their speech a bit. This is what you want to do when you are talking to your pup. You can forget about all of that baby talk nonsense where you start asking if Spotty-wotty-baby wants to go on walkie. You can use full, regular words when you are talking to your pup without you having to degrade down to full-blown baby gibberish. Use regular words, but try to make them short when you use this tone.

Rewards Versus Punishment

Finally, one last thing to remember when you are training your puppy is that you need to remember the difference between punishment and rewarding. When you focus on being rewarding for good behavior, you are much more likely to encourage those good behaviors that you want to see in your pup. You are much more likely to get your pup to go along with you and what you are wanting to do if your pup can see that he or she is likely to get a reward for those good behaviors.

*W*hen you focus on making sure that behaviors that you like are rewarded, you encourage your pup to repeat them again and again. Your pup will see that those behaviors were worthwhile because they led to both of you getting exactly what you wanted out of the situation. You are happy, which is a reward for your pup on its own, but you also offered your pup some sort of reward or treat for doing what he should have done. That encourages your pup further in the future to repeat those behaviors. You should always work on rewarding the positive to encourage those behaviors more in the future rather than making them neutral. You want your pup to feel driven to performing those behaviors because those behaviors are the ones that you want to see.

*P*unishment does not teach the pup what to do—it teaches the pup what *not* to do, which is exceedingly vague. Imagine that you walk into a room and there is a strange item that you have never seen before sitting on a table and you are told to use it. You may not know what it is or what it is for. Now, imagine that you ask them what it is meant for. They then tell you what it is *not* for, without ever specifying what you should do with it. Do you know what you should be doing now?

. . .

*T*he chances are, no. You do not know what you should be doing with it. You have no idea what it is that you need to do with it and being told what else not to do did not help you get any closer to figuring out that proper behavior. You see this oftentimes with people using the command, "No." You may know that the command is good for telling someone to stop doing what they are doing, but for a dog, they are confused. They need you to specify what you want them to do, and punishing the behaviors that are wrong does not help them.

HOUSEBREAKING YOUR PUPPY

NEXT, it is time to look into housebreaking your puppy. Puppies are not born knowing that they can only relieve themselves outside. However, they do have a natural inclination to avoid going in their beds. This can, unfortunately, end with your own bed being used as a potential area to relieve himself, if you do not train him, but thankfully, there are methods that you can learn to help eliminate those negative behaviors entirely.

*W*ithin this chapter, we are going to be diving into how to housebreak your puppy. No one wants to have puppy pee and poo all over their home, so you will probably find that this is one of the first training exercises that you are going to be regularly pushing. You want to ensure that your pup is not going to have accidents all over your house, but you may not know where to begin. Thankfully, however, your resource for potty training or housebreaking your dog is here.

. . .

What to Expect

Before you begin, please note that good potty training is not instantaneous—not even close. Potty training will take time, consistency, and patience. You cannot expect to see that your dog has become fully house trained for up to a year with some of the larger breeds that tend to develop a bit slower than their smaller counterparts. Because the various breeds of dogs are so incredibly different from pup to pup, it can be really difficult to know what to expect for your specific breed. This means that you may want to stop right now and go to look up a specific guide for you. This chapter is going to be going over the basics that are going to apply for just about any dog, but if you want specifics, you will need a book dedicated to your breed.

When you begin, you are going to find that you will need to take your pup out regularly. Smaller breeds will need to go out much more frequently than larger breeds just due to being smaller and therefore having smaller bladders and higher metabolisms. Both of these translate to going regularly. Larger breeds may be able to go just a bit longer than their smaller counterparts, but not by much during those early years.

As a general rule, a pup can hold its bladder for roughly one hour per year of age, plus one. We have already discussed this. However, in theory, that means that your 3-month-old dog will need you to take him out every four hours, even overnight when you may otherwise want to be sleeping. You will need to do this to meet your pup's biological need to relieve itself.

. . .

*I*n potty training, you are going to be best served learning to recognize your pet's cues and then taking him out every time you see them. Every time your pup does go outside, you will want to praise him or her heavily. You may even decide to tie some high-value treats to this activity—perhaps your pup gets a treat out of your pocket each time that he or she goes outside. In making sure that you are regularly reinforcing this behavior, you will find that your pup is much happier to go outside over time.

*H*ow to Housebreak Your Puppy

Housebreaking your puppy is quite simple—it will just take lots of time, patience, and reinforcement before your pup entirely catches onto the process. All you have to do is follow the following steps:

- Keep your pup on a schedule regularly—there should be food at very specific times each day and then remove it when that time is up. This will help regulate out his or her metabolism.

- Take your pup out first thing in the morning and every hour during the time that you are potty training. Your pup may be able to hold it for longer, but it will not help him or her really train any better if you do and you run the risk of having more and more accidents that you are trying to avoid.

37

- Make sure that pup goes out right before bed each and every night.

- Take the pup to the same place in your yard each tie and encourage him or her to sniff around. The smell of previous waste will linger and encourage him to go there again. This is precisely why so many pups will have the same accident in the same places indoors—they can smell their waste there.

- Always praise when your pup goes outside, followed by a high-ticket treat at first. You may try going on a walk, for example, or playing with your pup after he or she has gone.

Crate Training

Some people find that they are happiest using a crate to train their pups to go. This is because being confined in a crate activates your pup's natural instincts—they will not void where they sleep, and because you will be encouraging them to sleep in their crate, they are not likely to have accidents in there if they can avoid it at all. You will want to ensure that your pup is going out regularly, even if you keep him or her in a crate, and if you are crating, make sure that they are never in there longer than a couple of hours at a time.

. . .

$\mathcal{W}$ith crate training, all you are going to do is place your pup in the crate for naps and when you are not actively supervising him or her. This can really help you make sure that there are no accidents around the house. When you are crate training, keep the following factors in mind:

- Make sure that your pup has enough room to stand up, turn around, and lie down comfortably. However, there should not be enough room for your pup to use a corner as a potty spot. There are crates that you can get that are entirely adjustable—you will be able to change the sizes of the siding to accommodate your pup over time so you do not have to keep buying new ones.

- If your pup is going to be crated longer than an hour or two, you must ensure that there is a freshwater dispenser present for him or her to get fresh water whenever necessary.

- If you are not home during the potty-training period, make sure that you make arrangements for someone to come in and relieve your pup if you cannot get home. For example, if you work so you cannot get home every three or four hours, try asking a neighbor if they can keep an eye on your pup. You may be surprised to find that they are totally happy to do so.

- Discontinue this method if you find that your pup regularly relieves himself in the crate. You may have a crate that is too big and your pup is not learning.

Umbilical Training

Some people find that the best way they can train their pup to avoid accidents is a method known as umbilical training. This is exactly what it sounds like—you will want to make sure that you tether yourself to your pup so your pup cannot get up and cause trouble elsewhere. You will primarily be doing this by using a leash. At first, you may find that this is inconvenient, but over time, you may come to realize that this is actually incredibly useful to you—you will be able to use this method to ensure that your pup is not out of your sight long enough to have an accident, and you will be able to respond to your pup immediately if you do see that he is getting ready to go.

When you do this, you will want to make the leash a decent length, but not long enough that your pup can slip away and out of sight. You will want to ensure that your pup is close enough that you can see him at all times. Beyond that, you simply keep your dog at your side. There is not much else to it beyond that—you just keep your pup with you as much as possible.

. . .

*I*f your pup is resistant at first, don't give in. If he has had his freedom for a while, he may assume that he can, in fact, still be given free rein to wander as he wishes. However, that is not going to work for you—you need to be able to see him to immediately get him out. If you do find that he is starting to go outside only and accidents are no longer happening, then it could be time to let him have some more autonomy. However, any time that he starts to have accidents again, he will need to be tethered to you again.

*U*sing a Bell at the Door

Some people like to train their pups to ring a doorbell when they need to go out. This allows them to sort of communicate or convey what it is that they need at any given moment. One of the best ways to do so is to get a strip of fabric or a thick rope and attach some bells to it. Then, place the bells on a hook next to the front door, low enough that your pup can reach them. Every time that you are going to go out with your pup to take him out, ring the bell. Over time, he will start to associate that sound of the bell ringing with you cuing to him that it is potty time. Over time, he will get better and better at this and he will be able to ring the bell himself when he needs to go.

*T*he trick here, however, is that you have to believe him. If he rings the bell, you go outside to let him out. You will have to do it every time so he learns the message—he learns that if he rings the bell, he gets to go to his potty spot.

TEACHING YOUR PUPPY TO FOLLOW COMMANDS

ULTIMATELY, training your puppy to follow commands is all about repetition and modeling. Over time, your pup will learn to begin to follow your commands. Training can be quite tricky to those that have never done it—pups do not inherently understand what you mean when you tell them to sit. It has to be learned over time and that can be quite tricky sometimes. We are going to go over the general process of training your pup in this chapter, going step by step to see what you need to do and what your pup will likely do at each and every step along the way.

Timeline for Training Your Pup

Training your pup can begin as soon as you have him home with you. While your pup is not going to have much in the way of an attention span yet, you are going to find that he is quite eager to please. During this juvenile stage, you are going to be teaching simple commands. You really are not working much more than teaching the rules of the house, what your pup can expect from you, and how you are going to interact with him or her. This is simple enough. This stage of training will be all about how you can interact with your pup in a gentle, positive manner and how likely you are to ensure that he or she is going to receive that message that you were trying to convey without a problem. This is more like encouraging your pup when they do happen to do what they want. You may be using treats to sort of guide the behavior, but you are not able to get them to truly understand it yet. This is like the foundation for the training that will come soon.

*I*t is not until later, when your pup is around 6 months of age that he or she will be ready for proper, formal training. This is when you can start the processes of training all of the commands that you would really like to do. This is where you will be using the proper stages that will be introduced shortly and that you will be able to expect your dog to follow on a regular basis. These different steps that you will go through will be to introduce the command, reward the command when your pup gets it right, practice and reinforce the command, and then remembering to continue to train the command and use it regularly to ensure that it is not forgotten.

*I*ntroduce the Command

The first stage here is going to be introducing the command—you are going to be deciding which command that you want your pup to know and then stating that command out loud. Especially in the early days, then, you are going to facilitate getting the pup to move into the way that you are trying to get him to. If you want to, for example, train your pup to sit, you may say, "Sit." Immediately afterward, you then use a piece of food to entice your pup to shift into a proper sitting position. You would do this simply by moving the piece of food in front of him until he looks up at it, and then continue moving it behind him. You will sort of coerce him into flopping down on his bottom in a sitting position. You will want to make sure that you only state the command once when you are trying to get the pup to obey.

Reward the Command

As soon as the pup is in the right position, it is time to reinforce it—you do this through positively rewarding the pup for doing the right thing. You give him the food, praise him, and pet him. His mind has now connected the word that you said, the food, and the positive feelings all to that behavior that you are trying to train, and that is where the power is going to be coming from.

When you reward the command, you want to make sure that your pup is rewarded with something that is going to be desirable. Over time, however, you will begin to fade out the food as a reward for following through with the behavior. You may find that what works for you is a gesture along with the treat so the gesture gets paired in there, too. No matter what the command, however, you always want to make sure that you reward it, even when it is a basic one and your pup is fully grown. You can do this with a quick verbal affirmation and a pat on the head.

Practice the Command

Next comes practice. When it is time to practice those behaviors, you are putting the mall to good use and ensuring that the pup starts to connect the word that you are using to the action that you are asking for. This is done with patience and careful encouragement. Over time, however, you will find that your pup is quite eager to follow along. Your pup will be happy to give you the result you wanted if you are willing to reward him.

*P*ractice will happen over a long period of time. Some commands may not take very much at all to reinforce but other more complex commands, such as trying to train a trick that has no real purpose other than entertainment, like playing dead in response to finger guns, will most likely take your pup much longer to figure out.

*R*einforce the Command

Reinforcement will be an important step for you. Each and every time you find that your pup is doing what you have commanded, you must make sure that you reinforce it. You can do this with anything that you want to do. All that matters is that you are making sure that your pup is catching onto your expectations and that you are making sure that your pup is interested in continuing to follow them.

*C*ontinue Use of the Command

Finally, the last step to training your pup is ensuring that he is exposed to continued use of these commands as you continue to practice them. You want to ensure that your pup knows what you want. You also want to make sure that the automatic response between your command and the action will happen regularly without much of a problem. When you do this, you will find that you will actively be encouraging your pup to remember this command.

*E*very time you repeat the command in different contexts, you will find that you are encouraging him or her to continue to remember the command. You are strengthening that connection in your mind and in doing so, you will find that you will naturally get your pup to follow along with what you want.

*W*hen you first start training, you probably chose to do so in an environment that was not particularly distracting. It could have been at your home, for example, where there is not much going on. However, at some point, you will really need to reinforce that command by practicing it in a busier setting as well. You will need your pup to know to stop and listen to you, no matter where you are or what you are doing, and because of that, you have to be able to train your pup under many different settings, reinforcing it as much as you can.

COMMANDS YOUR PUPPY NEEDS TO KNOW

AT THIS POINT, we are going to go over several of the most important commands that your pup needs to know. These commands are going to ensure that your pup is the best-behaved puppy citizen he or she can be, and that is important. Remember, a well-trained pup is a happy, healthy, safe pup, so even if you may find that the effort is a lot, it is absolutely worth it in the end. If you are not in a good place to train your pup, you may find that you are better off attempting to find someone who can. Thankfully, dog trainers are able to be found just about anywhere you go these days, so you can probably find some way to outsource the work without much trouble.

"Sit"

Perhaps the most basic command your pup can learn is the sit command. This will tell your pup to stop, plop his bottom down, and pay attention. We have already gone over the basics of this one. You will repeat the word, sit, and then take a treat right next to his nose, which you will then move up. He will follow the treat, and you will then continue to move it back. Your pup will naturally sit down when he pulls his head too far back, and at that point, you will want to shower him with all of the praise he deserves.

"Watch Me"

This command tells your pup to stop and look at you—ultimately, your pup should look to you every time that he or she is unsure what to do because you are going to be the one making that decision. This is the attention command. To do this, you are going to repeat the phrase of your choice and then offer a high ticket treat to your pup. You will start at your pup's nose with the treat and then bring it closer to yourself. Your pup should naturally follow the treat and will eventually make eye contact with you. At the eye contact, offer the treat.

"Down"

Down is a tough command to teach due to the fact that lying down is naturally a passive position to be in. They do not like being in vulnerable positions often, so you will have to work for this one. Usually, you are going to want to take a treat that smells good and show it to your pup, let your pup sniff it and then drop your hand, still holding the treat down to the floor. Slowly shift your hand away from the pup, dragging it closer to you while the up continues to sniff at the treat. As you do so, the pup will slowly follow along and you will wind up with a puppy that is eventually lying down on the floor. As soon as the pup's belly is on the floor, you say, "Down," and then offer the treat to him to reinforce it.

. . .

"Stay"

Next comes the stay command. This is incredibly important to be able to use—it tells your puppy to stop whatever he is doing and remain put. This is started by telling your pup to sit first. Your pup will naturally sit. Then, showing the treat to your pup, you will take a step backwards while repeating, "Stay." Take a few steps back. If the pup tries to get up to follow you, quickly tell him no and then move back further. Over time, you will reinforce the idea that your pup must stay put. This particular command will require a lot of reinforcement several times a day.

"Come"

The next command to work on with your pup is telling him to come along with you. This is done quite simply—put your pup in a collar and a leash and make sure that you have a treat in your hand. Say your command and pull your pup's leash a little bit. As soon as he moves forward, you then give him the treat. You will want to do this regularly as well, encouraging your pup to come on command. Eventually, you will want to try in different contexts, such as without a leash or outside.

"Drop It"

One last basic command that you may find that you need your pup to learn is to learn how to drop something on command. Whether your pup will have found an unsavory object outside, has stolen a shoe, or done anything else, you will want to make sure that your pup will let go if you tell him to. This is done by taking something that your pup likes. Perhaps you have your pup's favorite toy. Encourage your pup to take the toy in his or her mouth and then pull at it. Let your pup have it. Then, find another object that you know that your pup likes and offer that one instead. When your pup drops the first item that was in its mouth, you repeat your command and then offer the treat. This will have to be repeated regularly to get your pup to master it, but it is perhaps one of the most important. When you can tell your pup to drop something and have them do so without thinking about it, you will be able to get them to release items that they should not have. Should you find that your pup is chewing on your pants leg, you can tell your pup to drop it, and he should.

TRAINING TRICKS

WHEN YOU HAVE MASTERED some of the most basic commands that your pup can learn, you may find that you are ready to move onto something that is a bit more entertaining. You may realize that your pup loves to learn, so long as you have the right environment to facilitate it, so you decide to train some tricks.

*L*argely, these are going to be trained the same way that you would train commands. They really are no different—the only difference is that the tricks that you train are likely to be entertaining rather than functional commands that are necessary for controlling your pup. People have all sorts of reasons that they may decide to train tricks. They may find them funny or they may find them a great way to bond with their animals. No matter the reasons that you have chosen, however, you should have fun and treat them the same way that you would a command. Now, let's go over a few common tricks.

. . .

Shake Hands

Shaking hands is quite easy to teach on command. All you have to do is make sure that you have plenty of treats on hand and the patience to walk through the process. The only command that your pup needs to know at this point is to sit down for you.

Start by instructing your pup to sit. As you do so, hold a treat in one hand, showing it to your pup. Then, close your hand so it is out of sight. Then, tell your pup, "Shake." You should then move your own fist underneath the dog's nose. He will be able to smell the treat and will most likely want it. He will most likely sniff at your paw and after a few moments, he will use his paw to touch yours. He will be trying to dig the treat out. When your pup's paw touches your hand, you then offer the treat and say, "Good."

This trick can be great for entertaining your pup, kids, and just about anyone else. It looks cool, but is not going to do much else for you beyond that. However, you may find that it is great mental stimulation for a pup that needs to be kept busy. Remember, just as with all other commands, you must make sure that your pup is getting your undivided attention and is getting reinforced regularly. You will want to repeat this process several times a day over the course of several weeks. Over time, you will find that your pet will pick up on it.

. . .

*A*fter time, you can command your pup to shake and stop offering the treat as often. You can switch the hand in which you offer the treat, for example, to start removing that association that touching the hand that was offered out is enough to get the treat. Eventually, you should be able to give the command without any real reinforcement at all.

Roll Over

Another common trick that people love is telling their pup to roll over. It is a great way to entertain children in particular, and could be a great way to help your child bond with your dog. All you will need to do this is teach your pup how to lay down. If you have that down, then the next steps will be simple.

*W*ith your pup lying down in front of you, you will want to kneel in front of him. Make sure that you have a treat in your hand as you do so. Hold the treat near his nose, but to the side somewhat. He will naturally start to sniff at the treat in your hand. Then, you are going to want to move your hand slowly, with him continuing to follow it in your hand. Move it to his shoulder and you should see him roll onto his side. Praise him at this step and offer the treat at this point in time. You are not done with the complete trick yet, but this is a great point to keep moving from.

*A*fter a few days when your pup has this particular motion down, you can then begin to continue the movement. You should no longer stop right at the shoulder but should go all the way to the backbone. He will most likely roll onto his back, at which point, you keep going until you get to the floor on the other side. He should roll all the way over at that point. Give him the treat and praise.

When he will consistently roll all the way over, you can then introduce the command that you are trying to add as well. You will have your pup perform the whole motion, then say, "Roll over," when you give him the treat, followed by praise.

Over time, you will want to gradually phase out the treat and the hand motion. You may first start by eliminating the treat, and slowly then cut out the motion as well, leaving only the verbal command behind.

CORRECTING COMMON BEHAVIORAL PROBLEMS

Now, despite the cuteness of your pup, you are most likely going to find that there will be some extra hurdles for you to get over along the way. This is to be expected—your pup will want to challenge you at some point. Pups test boundaries as they age, much like children do, and because of that, you can usually wind up with some annoying behaviors that will need to be created. You will need to be able to correct these behaviors if you hope to be successful at training your pup and because of that, you may find that you need some help.

*W*ithin this chapter, we are going to go over some of the most common puppy behavioral problems that you are going to encounter, as well as how to cut down on them. Some pups will be harder than others, but if you do learn how to defeat those behaviors, you and your pup will be able to live in harmony.

. . .

*N*ipping

Pups don't have hands that they can use to explore the world around them, and they wind up using their mouths instead. This may be cute at first when you have a little pup that can't do much damage, but as your puppy grows in those sharp teeth, people can get hurt. Your pup is not trying to hurt you—but you do need to teach your pup that biting and nipping is not an appropriate form of play.

*F*or young pups, you can defeat this relatively simply—start playing with your pup and let him take your hand in his mouth. As soon as he starts to bite hard enough for you to want him to stop, suddenly make a loud, high-pitched yelping sound. When you do this, you are conveying that you were hurt. Then, let your hand go limp altogether. Your pup will think that you have been hurt and because of that, he may start to lick you to help you feel a bit better. When he stops biting and starts to lick, offer praise and then continue to play.

*I*f, after around 15 minutes, he continues to nip often, more than 3 times, you may find that you need to stop playing. Yelp and turn away altogether, ignoring him for a few seconds .When you do this, he will realize that he has been ignored and it will catch him off guard. He will feel bad and he will want to re-engage with you. After 20 seconds or show, you can start to play again.

. . .

*R*epeat this process of yelping and stopping every single time he nips too hard.

*C*hewing

Chewing is another common problem. This particular one, however, is not out of maliciousness or even being poorly behaved. Your pup is teething, and wants to chew on something. Rather than cutting out all chewing, you are going to want to make sure that your pup learns what is acceptable to chew on and what is not. This means that you will give him something that he is allowed to chew on that is entirely different from everything else around him—he should see that it is something that is distinguished from other items and entirely unique. If you use a shoe or another item that looks like another common household item, you run the risk of teaching him to look at those other similar items to chew on as well, which is not at all what you are going for right now.

*W*hile you are trying to train your pup what is acceptable, make sure that he is kept on a short leash, perhaps tethered to you, when you cannot supervise. Beyond that, make sure that he is getting plenty of exercise and going out regularly. When you do catch him chewing on something, stop him and redirect to something that he is allowed to chew on. You will want to do so by stamping your feet or clapping to startle him to make him stop before finally replacing what he was chewing on with the chew toy.

. . .

*J*umping

Puppies love us and when we come home from being away for a while, they want to say hi. They jump up to get a good smell of you and to figure out where you have been. However, as your pup gets bigger, this gets dangerous and turns into a big problem that you will need to eliminate. This means that you need to figure out how to teach your pup that all feet need to be on the ground.

*D*oing so will require you to be persistent, but is quite easy. When you walk in the door, instead of getting down for your pup to sniff at you, try entirely ignoring your pup. You will essentially tell your pup that you are not offering any positive attention until he is calm. When he is calm, you can then shower him with all of that affection that you know he wanted in the first place. You just want him to know that he cannot take it by climbing onto you.

*W*hining

Puppy whining may be cute at first, until it never stops. Whining is ultimately your pup's way of asking for help. He wants or needs something and is trying to get that in any way that he can. He may have lost his toy under the couch. He may be bored, or he may want attention. If you hear your pup whining, it would be a good idea to investigate to see if there is an easy solution. Whining makes sense if your pup needs to go out, is hungry, or needs help getting something. However, if there are no good reasons, he may be whining just to get your attention, and that is bad.

. . .

*W*hen you want to eliminate this sort of whining for your attention, then, what you are going to want to do is eliminate giving it to him altogether. He will no longer be allowed to have your attention when he whines at you. If he still does not stop whining, calmly tell him to be quiet. He may not stop right away, especially if you have not taught that as a command. Eventually, you may have to sort of snap at him—using a louder tone to make him feel like he was scolded for the whining—and then stop paying any attention to him at all.

*H*aving Indoor Accidents

Indoor accidents are something that no one wants to deal with, but are ultimately, an unavoidable part of owning a pet. When you are dealing with indoor accidents, you may feel frustrated about it. However, stop and make sure that you are firstly taking your pup out as much as possible. Make sure that you also are able to clean up the spot with a good enzyme cleaner to get as much of the smell out as possible to ensure that the scent is entirely eliminated.

*P*ups, when they can smell where they have gone before, will continue to go there because they think that is an okay place—otherwise, why would they be able to smell it? When you use a good enzyme cleaner, however, you can destroy those scents altogether. You can find these online and at your local pet store—try to find one that will work for you and you will not be disappointed. These cleaners can be used to eliminate all sorts of bacteria and stenches that you may not have even realized were there. You may even find that you will need to clean the entire floor with such a cleaner to see if there is some scent there that has been missed.

CONCLUSION

And with that, we have made it to the end of *How to Train a Puppy*. It has been a long journey, but this is really only the first step of your journey of a lifetime with your pup. You have the ability to mold your pup into developing the behavior that you would like to see from him and because of that, you should absolutely be able to enjoy your time with your pup. You can make sure that he is able to behave himself well and to ensure that you are not running into all of those bad habits that all too many dogs wind up developing somewhere along the way.

From here, all that is left is for you to put this information into use. It is no longer practice, but rather, it is solid, firm action that you need to make sure to utilize if you want to see results. Your pup, just as a child would, requires guidance. You need to be able to give your puppy the attention and guidance that he will need, and you now have the tools to do so.

Good luck on your journey into training your pup on how to behave—you should have the tools to at least get you started on the right foot! Remember, look into breed-specific resources, as this was largely a general guide for you. Finally, if you have found that this book was useful to you in any way or that the tips and tricks included within it are helping you train your new canine companion, please head over to Amazon to leave a review! It is always great to get all of that feedback.

MASTER DOG TRAINING

A Dog Training Guide for Beginners

Kenneth Binmoeller

INTRODUCTION

Welcome to *Master Dog Training*. If you purchased this book, you have either just adopted a dog, or you are planning on doing so. Bringing a dog into your life is a lot more work than people usually imagine, so picking up this book to learn more about how you can help your dog is the responsible thing to do.

Dogs in different stages of life require their own training techniques and execution. This may be obvious to some, but if you didn't already know this, understanding what your dog's age brings to the table is an important factor in delivering the right training techniques and execution. If you have no idea what different life stages bring to the table, don't worry, this book has got you covered.

Properly training your dog is crucial when it comes to building a close and successful relationship with your dog. Without the right training, dogs can develop bad behaviors that make it very hard for the two of you to coexist. Moreover, training your dog is crucial when it comes to the safety of you, your dog, and other people.

Training doesn't only mean teaching your dog how to sit, stay, or leave it. It also means enforcing good household behaviors, walking practices and in some cases, advanced level training to save lives or serve a purpose.

In this book, I will be covering all topics from teaching you the basics of the different dog life stages all the way to teaching you beginner to expert level dog commands. I will start off by teaching you about what to expect in a dog's puppyhood, adulthood, and seniorhood. I will teach you how to choose the right type of training and execution for your dog based on your dog's age, breed and your own individual lifestyle. Another important topic that I will be teaching you about is basic dog care. Properly taking care of your dog will reduce the chances of your dog exhibiting undesirable behaviors. After we cover those topics, I will move on to teach you about the different types of dog/puppy training, how to understand dog behavior and teaching you about various dog training techniques. At this point in the book, you should have an idea of what type of training you'd like to use for your specific dog and all the things you need to consider. Near the end of this book, I will teach you about more advanced level topics such as correcting behavioral problems, training your dog for public situations and learning about the numerous dog commands you can teach your dog.

There is a lot to take in, so get excited. The relationship between man and dog is one that lasts for a lifetime. Be ready to put in the work and I promise you the relationship will be a fulfilling one. So let's not wait any longer, let's start learning!

UNDERSTANDING THE STAGES OF A DOG'S LIFE

A HUGE PART of choosing the right training techniques and methods for your dog is to base it on the age of your dog. For instance, puppies learn very quickly, so they are able to adapt to any type of training technique very quickly. Adult dogs learn less quickly but they are more emotionally mature so they have a longer attention span for training sessions. Understanding the age of your dog and what comes with it will help you figure out what training types work best with your specific companion. I will break the dog's lifestyle for you starting from the different stages of puppyhood all the way to seniorhood.

Puppyhood

Everyone knows that puppies are incredibly cute. They literally grow before your eyes, and it is extremely fascinating! You get to watch your puppy learn, grow, and practice their new abilities. However, they can also be extremely needy, tiring, and relentless. People who decide to bring home a puppy need to have extreme patience during the first few months of your pup's life.

· · ·

*P*uppies start learning instantly at birth. The most receptive time for puppies to learn is between 2 - 4 months old. Like we mentioned in the previous chapter, this is the most important time to begin socializing them in order to prevent skittishness or fearfulness in the future. Responsible dog owners should be actively socializing their puppy at this age and begin house training.

*P*uppies require a lot of attention, especially during the initial weeks of bringing them home. They eliminate more frequently when they are younger so you have to take them outside often in order to potty train them. After the initial few weeks, they should learn some control and elimination should shrink down to 5 - 8 times a day.

*M*ake sure you are feeding your puppy high-quality puppy food that has the necessary nutrients. Avoid feeding your puppy human food as it imbalances the growth of bones, muscles, and organs. Puppies normally need to be fed four meals a day until they are three months old, where you can now feed them three meals a day.

*O*ther characteristics of puppies include the tendency for destructive chewing. In the world of dog body language, chewing strengthens teeth and is a form of mental stimulation. It is a puppy's way of learning about their environment and the world. Make sure to give your puppy plenty of chew toys to play with so they don't end up destroying your favorite pair of shoes. You should also begin to train them at this time what is appropriate to chew on and what isn't.

Neonatal Stage (0 – 2 weeks)

From when a puppy is born until two weeks old, they are 100% dependent on their mother for food and care. The mother will feed them using her breast milk and will care for them by making sure they are clean. Neonates are blind and deaf at birth but have a sense of touch and taste. Their movement is very limited and is only capable of a very slow crawl.

Transitional Stage (2 – 4 weeks)

When a puppy is two to four weeks old, they begin to interact with the rest of the litter as well as their mother. Their eyes open around the one month mark, and their sense of hearing and smell begins to develop more. During this stage, the puppy's teeth begin to emerge and they are able to slowly walk around and wag their tails. By the one month mark, the puppies should be able to eliminate waste without their mother's help.

Puppies also begin to wean around the one month mark. Usually, at the three-week mark, puppies begin to eat solid food instead of breastmilk. At this age, you can begin to offer the puppy wet food in small amounts.

Socialization Stage (4 – 6 weeks)

When the puppy is at the age of 1 to 1.5 months, they are still heavily influenced by their mother and littermates. They begin to play with each other learning social skills from the other pups and their mother. They learn skills like inhibited biting (play biting and not biting to hurt), group structure, and ranking. The puppies should be more vocal during this time frame; you may notice this through its growling or play barking.

Training Stage (6 – 8 weeks)

At this age, puppies are still learning socialization skills are not separated from their mother and siblings yet. You can begin to train your puppy as early as the 5-week mark, but they still need to be around their mother. At the 6 week mark, you can begin to introduce in-home training to your pup. You can begin to introduce a collar to him/her and encourage the use of his/her name. You may even begin rewarding your pup with treats and/or praise. You can begin to use training techniques such as positive reinforcement and clicker training (you will learn these methods later on in this book).

*A*t the two month mark, your puppy will start experiencing fear. Regular everyday objects and experiences may frighten them. This is perfectly normal and is not an indication that you will have a fearful dog. Avoid socializing your pup with other pups outside the litter or other household pets like cats before they have been vaccinated. This is to avoid picking up diseases like hepatitis that is fatal to all puppies.

*E*xtended Training Stage (8 – 16 weeks)

In this stage, the puppy is not much different than at the 2-month mark. They are still being socialized and getting used to new environments. During this time is a good opportunity for the owner to train more extensively and begin reinforcing good habits. You may start training your puppy to go to the washroom outside and on their own. You may fully switch over to solid puppy food at this point.

Establishing Hierarchy Stage (16 – 24 weeks)

During this stage, your puppy begins to grow rapidly and exponentially. Although puppies are naturally very energetic, don't exercise your puppy too much at this stage as he/she can overexert him/herself. This is the stage where puppies begin to utilize ranking in their group hierarchy. They start testing where they fit in in a group. You may notice that your puppy may be experiencing another phase of fear that seems to have come from nowhere. Again, this is extremely normal, and you have nothing to worry about. This time frame is also when you might notice that your puppy is losing their teeth. You may come home one day to your puppy having a bloody mouth and loose teeth around your home. This is entirely normal and lasts from the four-month mark to 8-month mark. Try to prevent your puppy from swallowing their own teeth if possible.

Adolescent Stage (24 – 52 weeks)

Puppies between the ages of 6 - 12 months are at their adolescent stage. They are very rambunctious, so it is important to continue the training process and continue to socialize your dog with many types of environments. At this age, they should be vaccinated and ready to go out in public areas such as dog parks or the city streets. These six months are crucial when it comes to your puppy's training. Make sure you are training your puppy every single day to keep them in a routine. If you want, you may start training your puppy with more advanced training such as agility training.

Adulthood

When you think the excitement of puppyhood is over, think again! Adolescence for dogs is just as physically and mentally challenging for them as it is for us. Just like humans, dogs also go through puberty where they go through a series of hormonal changes. Dogs reach their adolescence between the ages of 6 months and 18 months. During this time, your dog is going through lots of growth spurts, which may cause them some mild pain. This is during the time where their permanent teeth come in so your dog will need plenty of chew toys to chew on to relieve the pressure in their jaw. Their baby coat also begins to fall off during this period and their adult hair will grow in. This means that there will be more shedding during this time.

*D*ogs in the adolescence reach their sexual maturity between the eighth month and their twelfth month. Neutering or spaying your dog before this time frame will alleviate almost every symptom that comes with sexual maturity. Specific to female dogs, this will eliminate their first heat. You may begin to notice that your female dog is more playful and excited around other male dogs. During this time if your dog isn't spayed, you have to be careful when you are letting them roam. They may accidentally get impregnated without your knowledge. Moreover, female dogs in their adolescence need to urinate more frequently. They also may develop aggressive behavior specifically towards other female dogs. Make sure you are continuing to train and reinforce good behavior in your dog to prevent unwanted actions and behavior.

*A*dolescent dogs will also begin to show new behavior, some that may seem aggressive on the surface. Their bodies begin producing testosterone at a higher level, which results in more extreme behavior. During this time, male dogs start holding other dogs responsible for their duty based on the dog social hierarchy. This can lead to fighting with other dogs. It takes time and training for male dogs to learn these new feelings and responsibilities. Another common problem in adolescent male dogs is marking. This can usually be prevented if your dog is neutered before they reach puberty or with proper training.

*I*f your adolescent dog is showing signs of destructive behavior, it is likely because of boredom or anxiety. Make sure to give your adolescent dog a lot of exercises to help reduce their energy level to prevent and destructive behavior. They need to be given lots of mental stimulation in order to be calmer at home. During a dog's adolescence is a good time to train them as they are still in the learning stages when it comes to people and other animals. At this age, your dog is able to distinguish people from the ones they know and the ones they don't know. Be patient with your dog during this important stage in life, and continue holding the same training standards to your dog.

Seniorhood

Did you know that older dogs tend to be happiest? This is because they have settled in happily to a familiar routine and can give all their time and attention to being affectionate. Just like adolescence, different breeds reach seniorhood at different times, but it is important for you to know when this will be for your dog as it typically means that your dog needs to change their diet, exercise, health, and nutrition. Your veterinarian should be able to let you know when your dog needs to begin making these changes.

 few common problems within senior dogs are:

73

- Eye problems: Conditions like cataracts and hamper vision occur in older dogs and can lead to blindness.
- Orthopedic problems: This a condition due to normal wear and tear in the bones and joints of your dog. Arthritis is common for dogs at this stage in life.
- Hip dysplasia: This condition makes it hard for your dog to walk or run. Medication or surgery are possible solutions depending on how severe the condition is.
- Hypothyroidism: This condition slows your dog down and often leads to obesity or heart problems. Make sure to take your senior dog to frequent check-ups as this can be detected with a simple blood test and is easily managed using medication.
- Cancer: Cancer is a common disease that can show up in all phases of a dog's life but is most commonly found in older dogs.

*A*s dogs get older, they may begin to exhibit signs of confusion and memory lapses. They may need to go to the bathroom more frequently because of declining bladder and kidney functions. If your dog was never neutered or spayed, there is a higher risk of infections or cancers in the reproductive organs. By keeping a close eye on your dog, you may begin to see signs of this early. Medications can be used to help tackle some of these problems. It is important to treat your dog gently during these times and don't try to induce too much change. Activities like jumping or vigorous running should be avoided to prevent injury, pain, and further deterioration.

. . .

*A*s your dog gets older, he/she may help with activities that used to be simple for them. Make sure to consult your vet regarding what resources you can tap into to help your dog have an easier life. Small adjustments can be made in your home to help your dog function normally as long as possible. Make sure to give your dog lots of affection and touch as this is one of the most loving times of his/her life.

HOW TO CHOOSE THE RIGHT
TRAINING FOR YOUR DOG

As I mentioned earlier, choosing the right training for your dog based on their age is extremely important. Additionally, you have to consider factors like your dog's breed, your home, and your lifestyle. For instance, if you have a breed of dog that is very high energy like a Border Collie and you are a busy city dweller who works 40 – 50 hours per week, you may require a different training system compared to someone who owns a bulldog. Determining these factors before jumping into training will make your life easier. In this chapter, we will be exploring several topics related to this. You will learn about the differences between puppy and dog training, how the age of a dog influences your training program and different approaches based on your dog's age, breed and your lifestyle.

Distinctions Between Puppy Training vs. Dog Training

You have probably heard the phrase, 'you can't teach an old dog new tricks.' Although most people believe this to be true, it isn't. The truth is that it is a little harder to teach an old dog new tricks but the reality is that the most impressionable window for a puppy is so small that if you miss it, they might as well be considered an old dog. What is most important in training a dog despite its age or life experience is reinforcement. You can teach a puppy all the tricks in the world but if you are not constantly reinforcing it, they will soon forget everything.

How Does Dog Age Affect Your Training Program?

In the previous chapter, you have learned the major differences throughout the three stages of a dog's life; puppyhood, adulthood, and seniorhood. It should be quite obvious to you now that these different stages will require different training approaches. Although the training techniques used are going to be more or less the same, you will need to adjust the way you deliver these techniques.

*P*uppies are much more impressionable than adult dogs, so you are able to teach them more in a shorter time frame. However, they tend to be forgetful and if you are not constantly reinforcing behaviors, they will forget them. On the other hand, adult dogs (especially if you adopted him/her) typically come already with a basic set of knowledge. They are likely already socialized so you don't have to spend as much time exposing new experiences to them but you can spend more time reinforcing the behaviors that you deem as desirable.

*W*hen it comes to adult dogs, if you aren't 100% sure about their history and what they know and don't know, the best thing to do is to get an idea of what they do know. Test important behavioral things like:

- Does your dog jump on people?
- Does your dog know how to walk on a leash?
- Does your dog jump on furniture?
- Does your dog beg for food?
- Does your dog go to the bathroom outside?
- Does your dog know the basic commands (sit, stay, down, leave it, come)?
- Does your dog know more advanced commands (rollover, play dead, stand)?

By learning what your dog already knows, you may then decipher what other behaviors and actions you want to teach your adult dog. Since adult dogs are less impressionable than puppies, it may take them longer to actually learn a cue or behavior, but it will be easier to reinforce as adult dogs are more consistent. Puppies are always doing an array of actions so it is difficult to positively reinforce the right things because they are jumping from action to action. If you are trying to teach your dog a new cue, make sure to schedule in training sessions multiple times a day. By doing consistent training, your dog will learn a lot faster and you can easily discover new traits and behaviors about them. Keep in mind to avoid harsh punishment during training. There is a lot of evidence regarding punishment towards the dog and how that is usually ineffective. Dogs respond best to positive reinforcement where a reward or praise is involved. Punishment, in this case, would be in the form of no reward, no praise, or no acknowledgment at all. You will learn more about the positive reinforcement technique in the later chapters of this book.

. . .

$\mathscr{I}$f your dog is older and is in his/her seniorhood, try to avoid training that is too intense. When it comes to older dogs, they are still very capable of learning, but because of their lower energy levels and weaker body, training sessions cannot be too vigorous. Instead, for older dogs, you should focus on reinforcing the already existing good behaviors to avoid deterioration. For example, older dogs tend to have more accidents inside the home due to weakened bladder and kidney functions. You can do more reinforcement by giving rewards and treats when your senior dog has successfully gone to the bathroom outside. Make sure to practice basic commands with your senior dog and continue to reward for every successful action. These basic commands are very useful when it comes to managing your dog and preventing bad behavior. For instance, if your senior dog becomes anxious in a certain situation and becomes aggressive, you can control their demeanor by commanding them to 'sit' or 'down.' The five basic commands i.e., extremely efficient in managing the behavior of a dog. By continuing to reinforce the basics to your senior dog, you will help make their retirement years easier for them and yourself.

What Is the Biggest Difference Between Training A Puppy Compared to a Dog?

If you haven't yet adopted a dog, you are likely debating between getting a new puppy or adopting an adult/older dog. There are definitely many things to consider; this chapter should help you with your decision. Although there isn't one choice that's better than the other, there are still a lot of differences. Let's take a look at the major ones that relate to training the most:

- Puppies are a lot of work compared to adult dogs. Puppies need to be trained from scratch and to learn what is good behavior and what isn't. On top of the extensive training, they require a lot of socialization with other people and animals so that she does not grow up to be skittish and fearful of the world. As he/she grows (and there is a lot of growing up to do), he/she will discover new things, make messes, and have many accidents. A lot of people are surprised at how much work actually comes with a puppy.

- Puppies' health and size tend to be more unpredictable than adult dogs. Puppies who are adopted from shelters tend to come from not ideal situations. This means that we don't have a lot of crucial information regarding their parents to identify pre-existing health conditions or temperament problems. Puppies with hidden conditions may require special training or attention that unsuspecting owners don't realize.

- Puppies that are from shelters typically lacked veterinarian attention prior to arriving there. Shelters normally provide medical care, vaccinations, and treatment against disease. However, it is likely that the puppy has not experienced much besides the shelter itself, and behavioral problems won't show up until they reach their new home. This will require more vigorous training to make sure the puppy is properly trained and acclimated to the new home.

- Adult and senior dogs are emotionally mature already. This means that there is less likelihood of aggression or other undesirable behavioral problems. This does not mean that adult dogs don't require training; it just means that they have likely been exposed to many things which will not require as much time and training to refine.

- Adult and senior dogs make great first time pets for new owners. Adult dogs tend to not require as much training as they already know the basics of house training and simple commands. If you are someone who cannot devote multiple months to train, socialize, and properly exercise a puppy, an adult dog is a great option. Rather than training everything from scratch, you can reinforce the good behaviors that your adult dog already has and simply just curb bad behavior.

- You know what you are getting into with an adult/senior dog. When you have an adult dog, you know what you are getting into just by interacting with them. You can see their physical traits and get a good sense of the dog's temperament. Although dogs that are in shelters don't typically show their true temperament until they are settled in a home, you still get a good general idea of where to begin in terms of training and reinforcement.
- Adult and senior dogs are just as loving as a puppy. If you are concerned that older dogs won't show as much affection as puppies, you are wrong. Dogs are very resilient and open-hearted creatures and are able to overcome their past in a matter of just a few days. Some may carry a bit more baggage than others, but with enough love, affection, and care - your dog will be loyal to you for the rest of his/her life.

If you haven't decided on a puppy, adult, or senior dog to adopt yet - the above comparisons should give you a better understanding of what to expect with each dog. I highly urge those who don't have that much time in their days away from getting a puppy as they are typically much more work than people realize. Lots of veterinarian and dog training professionals advise new owners of puppies to take several weeks off of work to properly have the time to train their puppy.

BASIC DOG CARE

TRAINING a dog isn't the whole journey. Learning to properly care for your dog is just as important as behavioral problems can arise if your dog's needs are neglected. Just like how training programs are different based on your dog's age and breed, dog care is different as well. For instance, puppies and dogs require different types of dog food based on nutrition. If your dog is a short-haired dog, you may not need to brush him/her as often as you would with a long-haired dog. Certain breeds are also more prone to diseases, so understanding the characteristics of the breed of dog you have will help you a lot in understanding what your dog care routine should be. In this chapter, I will be teaching you how to properly take care of your dog's hygiene, choosing the right food and feeding schedule, educating you on neutering/spaying practices and socializing your dog. Let's begin.

How Do I Choose What Food to Buy?

Nowadays, there is such a large variety of dog food available to purchase in the present day. How in the world are we supposed to choose the right brand? For starters, there are generic types of dog food brands and premium type foods. The premium dog food brands generally offer a higher nutritional density, so you are able to feed your dog less but achieve the same nutritional requirements. One major benefit of premium dog food is that their ingredients tend to be stable and does not vary much from batch to batch. Generic dog food brands are less strict on their ingredient compositions so each batch may be different.

*P*remium dog food companies are big investors in the nutritional research and product development department. They are always looking for innovative ways to upgrade their recipes, formulas, and cutting edge technologies. Premium dog food is a good option for the owners who want to stay on top of the industry and provide the healthiest option for their dog. However, this doesn't mean you should automatically buy any type of premium dog food out there. Dog owners are actually recommended to take their research one step further by researching and visiting the companies that make their dog food. A lot of the times, your local premium dog food company will offer tours or open houses of their factory and will give you a first-hand look into what goes into their products, how it's made, and where their ingredients come from. My personal recommendation is to choose the premium brands if you have the resources to do so. Typically, the premium brands use high-quality ingredients like premium cuts of meat or organic grains to make their food. Generic brands use more low-quality ingredients like leftover scraps of mixed meat or not pesticide-free ingredients.

. . .

*T*o make sure you are keeping your adult or senior dog healthy and happy, you have to make sure that their diet includes 37 specific nutrients. These nutrients all have to be intricately balanced across carbohydrates, proteins, vitamins, minerals, and fats and oils. You may have also noticed that there are different textures that dog food typically comes in. The differences are very large, so it is important to know which type is what. There are three types of dog food that you could serve to your dog. This includes:

- **Kibble**: This is a 100% dry food and the most common type of dog food found. It is more economical compared to the other two types of dog food and provides a complete balanced diet for dogs that come in all breeds, sizes, and ages. This is the recommended type of food for adult dogs as it helps keep their teeth and digestion system healthy.
- **Canned food**: This is a wet food that normally comes in the form of a can. It is the most expensive type of pet food, but dogs typically find this type to be the tastiest. Canned food is great for puppies that have not developed the teeth to chew up kibble properly or good for senior dogs that have weaker teeth and digestion. Since canned food is the most expensive type of food, most dog owners reserve them as a treat or on an as-needed basis.
- **Semi-moist food**: This type of food usually comes in single-serving packets and is not a very common type of food. Semi-moist food is not economical and serves very little purpose. This type of food is usually just used as a special treat for their dog.

*E*xperienced dog owners and veterinarians recommend feeding your dog kibble as it is the most beneficial out of all three types, especially if your dog is in its adulthood. Its hard texture creates the necessary friction in your dog's mouth when they chew that helps keep their teeth and gums healthy. If your dog is having trouble chewing up the hard kibble, you can add some water into the kibble to help soften it up. You can also decide to mix in some wet food with dry kibble to soften the texture. However, hard kibble without water is the best type of food to feed your adult dog as it is very effective in maintaining good dental hygiene.

Nutrition: What Do I Need Do I Consider?

If you have ever walked down an aisle of a pet store or even a department store, you probably have noticed the large variety of pet foods. As a new dog owner, it is easy to get overwhelmed by the number of options and specialized pet foods. Due to research, over the years it has definitely gotten more complicated when it comes to pet care. In the past, the variety of dog food options were much more limited. Even dog owners who were extremely responsible and knowledgeable didn't stress too much about what their dog food is made of.

*T*he process now seems to be a bit more difficult, but it is a good thing. Through many years of research using better ingredients and sourcing, new diet formulas have been created that lead to the better overall health of our dogs and puppies. Nowadays, you can find specialized dog food for puppies, adult dogs, senior dogs, diabetic dogs, or even diet dog food. Having a good understanding of what your puppy needs will give you a better idea of its nutritional needs and what foods can provide that. Not every dog is the same so if you have detailed concerns or questions, you should always consult your veterinarian for professional advice.

Puppy Feeding In the First Year

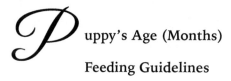uppy's Age (Months)

Feeding Guidelines

2-3 months

Puppies between the age of 2 months and 3 months should always be fed specialized puppy food to meet the needs for normal development. If you feed your puppy adult dog food, it will not provide the puppy with the necessary nutrients for good health. At this age, your pup should be fed four times a day to meet its nutritional demands. Bigger breeds should start to be fed unmoistened dry food by between month two and three, and for small dogs at month 3.

3-6 months

During this period, it is safe to decrease your feedings from four times a day to three times a day. Your pup should be losing its belly and chubbiness by month three. If your pup is still quite chubby and pudgy, continue to feed him/her puppy-sized portions until his/her body matures.

6-12 months

When your puppy reaches 6 months of age, you can decrease your feeding from three times a day to twice a day. This is around the time that you should be getting your dog spayed/neutered. Spaying and neutering lower the energy requirements of your pup, and this is when it is okay to switch from the nutrient-rich puppy food to adult dog food that maintains the nutrients. Smaller breeds can switch between month seven and month nine. Larger breeds typically switch at the one year mark. When in doubt, it is better to be on puppy food longer than less.

12 months +

At the age of one, most dog owners are recommended to continue feeding their dog twice a day but at half portions (1/2 portion total per day), but this is dependent on breed and metabolism.

*S*o how much food should I be giving my puppy? The answer is complicated as it is different based on what type of breed you have and its size. Portion sizes depend entirely on the dog's individual metabolism and body type. Nutritional value varies from dog to dog, just like humans. If your puppy occasionally misses a meal, you don't have to worry. It may mean that your pup is ready to have fewer feedings a day.

*B*elow is a generic puppy feeding chart that you can follow. You can determine how many cups you should be feeding your pup based on its age in months and its weight in pounds (lbs).

Generic Puppy Feeding Chart

WEIGHT OF PUPPY: AGE: 1 - 3 MONTHS

Age: 4 - 5 months
Age: 6 - 8 months
Age: 9 - 11 months
Age: 1 - 2 years
(lbs)
Cup(s) per Day
Cup(s) per Day
Cup(s) per Day
Cup(s) per Day
Cup(s) per Day
3 - 12 lbs
0.5 - 1 cup
0.6 - 1.25 cups
0.5 - 1.5 cups
Feed as an adult dog
Feed as an adult dog
13 - 20 lbs
0.5 - 1.25 cups
1.2 - 2 cups
0.75 cups - 1.3 cups
1 - 1.5 cups
Feed as an adult dog
21 - 50 lbs
0.5 - 1.5 cups
1.5 - 2.6 cups
1.2 - 2.3 cups
2 - 3 cups
2 - 4.25 cups
51 - 75 lbs
0.6 cups - 2.25 cups

1.5 - 4 cups

1.5 - 3.75 cups

2.5 - 4.75 cups

2.6 - 6.25 cups

76 - 100 lbs

1 - 2.5 cups

2.75 - 3.75 cups

2.75 cups - 6.3 cups

3.75 - 7 cups

5.6 - 11 cups

101 lbs +

2.5 cups + 0.3 cups for every 10 lb of body weight over 100 lbs

3.75 cups + 0.3 cups for every 10lb of body weight over 100 lbs

6.3 cups + 0.3 cups for every 10 lbs of body weight over 100 lbs

7 cups + 0.3 cups for every 10 lbs of body weight over 100 lbs

11 cups + 0.3 cups for every 10 lbs of body weight over 100 lbs

𝒶dult Dog Feeding Chart

Since breed, size, age, lifestyle, and health are all factors that play a role in how and what to feed your dog, it is important to consider all of them before purchasing dog food. For example, smaller breeds of dogs tend to have faster metabolisms. This means that they burn energy and calories at a higher rate. Depending on the specific dog and activity level, some dogs may even need to be fed twice the amount of calories than recommended. The best food formulas for smaller breeds are the ones that contain extra protein and are rich in carbohydrates and fats. This will be the nutrients that will give them the extra energy boost that they require. These types of food also come in smaller kibble size to match the smaller mouths and stomachs of the smaller breeds.

*O*n the contrary, larger breeds tend to have slower metabolisms, but they also have bigger appetites! They tend to make larger kibble sizes for large breed formulas to encourage the dog to chew for longer rather than inhaling their food. This type of dog formula has reduced fat and more concentrated protein to prevent weight gain.

*O*nce you have identified the ideal dog food that suits your dog's breed, age, size, and health, you faced with the next challenge: how much do I feed my dog and how many times per day? One of the most important parts to making sure your dog is healthy is feeding them the right amount of food. Too little or too much can cause a dog to suffer from nutritional deficiency and obesity-related health issues. Since each dog is dramatically different, there is no easy way to figure out how much a dog should be eating. When in doubt, always consult your veterinarian to make sure that the type and amount that you're feeding your dog is optimal. To give you a basic idea, I have included a recommended daily feeding chart for adult dogs that focus on four different breed sizes; toy, small, medium and large.

Recommended Daily Feeding For Adult Dogs

Size of Dog
Dog Weight
Cups Per Day

Toy
3 lbs
⅓ Cup (139 Calories)

6 lbs
½ Cup (233 calories)

10 lbs
¾ Cup (342 calories)
Small
15 lbs
1 cup (464 calories)

20 lbs
1 ⅓ cups (576 calories)

30 lbs
1 ¾ cups (781 calories)
Medium
40 lbs
2 ¼ cups (969 calories)

50 lbs

2 ⅔ cups (1145 calories)

60 lbs
3 cups (1313 calories)

70 lbs
3 ½ cups (1474 calories)
Large
80 lbs
3 ¾ cups (1629 calories)

90 lbs
4 ¼ cups (1779 calories)

100 lbs
4 ½ cups (1926 calories)

For every 10 pounds over 100 pounds of body weight, feed your dog an additional ⅓ cup.

. . .

These numbers are based on the total amount of calories that you should be feeding your dog over a 24-hour period. Most adult dogs are recommended to eat two meals a day, so you will need to divide the feeding amount by two and feed that amount twice a day. Make sure you are altering the amount you are feeding your dog based on your dog's lifestyle and their tendency for weight gain. Check your dog's weight every 2 - 4 weeks to keep track of whether they are losing weight or gaining weight. Then, adjust your portion sizes based on your results. Adult dogs who have a healthy weight typically have these traits:

- They have an hourglass figure when they are looked at from above. Their abdomen area should be narrower than their chest and hips.
- They look 'tucked up' from the side view. In other words, your dog's chest is lower to the ground than its belly when standing
- They have ribs that are not easily visible but can be felt with light pressure.

To help you understand what type of food you should be buying and portion size, I will use two case studies as an example.

Case Study #1:

So, let's use our knowledge plus the generic puppy feeding chart to calculate how much we need to feed our example dog, Charlie. Charlie is a 6-month-old dachshund. How often and how much dog food should we be feeding Charlie? First of all, since Charlie is only 6 months old, be sure to be using puppy food and not adult dog food. Secondly, let's do the math. According to the generic puppy chart, a dog at 6 months old and 10 pounds should be fed between 0.5 - 1.5 cups of puppy food a day. Since Trevor is on the higher range of the weight scale (3 - 12 pounds), we will round his puppy food intake to 1 cup a day. Dogs between 6 - 12 months of age should be fed in three feedings a day. Therefore, 1 cup/3 feedings means 0.33 cups per feeding.

*C*ase Study #2:

Smartie is a large Great Dane that weighs 110 lbs and is 8 years of age. He doesn't have any preexisting health conditions and loves to exercise. Smartie loves to eat and has a tendency to wolf down his food. What type of dog food and how much of it should we be feeding Smartie?

*S*ince Smartie is considered a very large dog due to his breed and his 110 lb weight. Since he doesn't have preexisting health conditions, he does not require a specialized diet dog food. However, he does have a tendency to wolf down his food, so we should be feeding Smartie specifically a large breed specialized dog feed that features large-sized kibble with the required nutrients. The large-sized kibble will encourage Smartie to chew his food before he can swallow it, which will prevent him from being able to wolf down his food. Next, we have to assess Smartie's weight. For every 10 lbs over 100 lbs, you are supposed to feed your dog an additional ⅓ cup. At 100 lbs, you are supposed to feed your dog 4 ½ cups. Therefore, at 110 lbs, the recommended amount would be 4 ⅚ cups (or approximately 4.8 cups). Since the recommended feedings for adult dogs are two feedings a day, you would need to divide the 4.8 cups by 2 which will give you 2.4 cups per feeding, twice a day.

Hygiene: What Does That Entail?

We have all encountered a few dogs in our lives that may not smell the best. Even though dogs are not expected to smell good 100% of the time, there is more to dog hygiene than just an occasional bath. You also have to look out for things such as brushing their teeth, cleaning their beds, and even cleaning their chew toys! If you are not paying attention to your dog's hygiene, you are increasing the possibility of your dog developing dental problems (e.g., teeth rot) or matted fur that could be very painful. Below is a list of items that are required for proper puppy hygiene.

Giving Your Dog/Puppy Baths

Did you know that a lot of dog owners actually over-bathe their dogs? This is the most common mistake as humans don't want a dirty dog lying in their bed or furniture. Shockingly enough, dogs don't need to be bathed often. Veterinarians actually recommend pet owners to bathe their dogs only once every three months. Dogs that are more active, have longer hair, or are constantly rolling in dirt can be bathed more frequently but an average dog will benefit from being bathed once every few months. Keep in mind that frequent bathing and washing can irritate your pup's skin and causing medical conditions like dandruff.

*L*earning how and where to wash your dog properly is important as well. Those who own smaller breeds of dogs have the advantage of just washing them in the sink or bathtub. However, if your dog is of a larger breed, obviously they can't fit in the sink. Portable doggy tubs are a good option if the weather is warm outside. If not, most pet stores actually offer a free dog washing station. Usually, this will consist of a large area with removable nozzles used to spray down your dog. Some people have the option of washing their dog in their yard with the garden hose. However, the water that comes out of your garden hose is likely cold, and unless it's really hot outside, your dog probably doesn't enjoy being bathed in ice-cold water.

So, how exactly do you wash your dog properly? This is important to learn so you don't go into the situation unprepared. Having a well-trained dog is important for this task as it is easiest when they are calm and sitting still. If your dog is not trained well, you may want to put them through behavioral training before taking on a task like this, especially if you have a dog of a large breed. Here are a few tips on how to bathe your pup properly:

- Brush your dog's hair/fur before the bath. Make sure your dog doesn't have any matted hair as it tends to hold lots of water. Washing your dog with matted hair will cause skin irritation. If you aren't able to brush or cut out those mats by yourself, it is recommended to take them to a professional groomer to have it done. Do not attempt to brush or cut out any mats if you aren't confident. Before you start the bath, you can put a large cotton ball in your dog's ear to help keep out water. This will prevent ear infections or irritations.
- Use lukewarm water for bathing your dog. Although humans typically shower with hot water, your dog's skin is different from ours. The water you use should not be

hotter than what you would use to wash a baby. Make sure that the water is not hot to touch but is a comfortable warmth. For larger breeds, keep the water even cooler as they overheat easily.

- Talk to your pet calmly during the bath. For dogs that are feisty during bath time, try to soothe them by talking to them gently. Don't yell, shout, or panic during this time as they may misunderstand the situation as being intimidating. After a few baths, they will learn that you are not trying to harm them and it can be quite an enjoyable experience.

- Use dog shampoo when bathing your dog. Dog shampoo dries out skin less than what human shampoo would. Lather the shampoo gently into your dog's body and massage it all over. Be careful not to get any shampoo in their eyes as it is extremely irritating.

- Rinse well. Make sure you are rinsing your dog until there are no more soap suds on its body. Any shampoo left on your dog's body after the bath can irritate its skin.

- Air dry your dog after the bath. Avoid using blow dryers to dry your dog's fur. Blow dryers tend to be too hot for a dog's skin. If needed, there are blow-dryers that are designed for dogs that you can purchase. These blow dryers expel air in lower temperatures that won't cause irritation.

- Reward your dog after the bath. Follow up the bath with lots of praise, petting, play, or treats. This will help your dog associate bath time to a reward, which will make them less irritable during the process. A lot of the times your dog may be frustrated after the bath so encouraging exercise afterward can help your dog blow off some steam.

*I*f you have a dog that is particularly bad with baths, you can explore the option of taking him/her to a professional groomer. If your dog requires a strenuous wrestle and a difficult struggle to keep him/her in the bath, it may be a better option to have a professional do it. Groomers will not only just give them a bath, but they will clip your puppy's nails, clean their buttocks area, trim hair near the eyes, and clean their ears as well. A lot of groomers are priced reasonably and do such a great job that you won't have to go back for another few months.

*I*f you have a dog that is a long hair breed like Poodles, Maltese, or Yorkies it is a 100% must to have them groomed by a professional. Since these breeds have hair and not fur, they don't shed their hair, and it keeps growing just like a human. Eventually, they will have to get it cut to make sure it doesn't dread. If you have a pup that has fur instead of hair, groomers are still helpful if your dog strongly dislikes baths. Groomers have the equipment and other professionals to help make the experience as smooth and as quick as possible. Overall, bathing is important to help keep your pup's skin and coat healthy, clean, and free of parasites. Depending on the breed and the environment you're in, some dogs may require more frequent baths. When in doubt, advise your local veterinarian to get a proper schedule on when and how often you should be bathing your dog.

Dental Care For Your Puppy/Dog

Did you know that the most common disease for dogs is not heartworms or rabies, but it is actually gum disease? Gum disease is formed in the dog's gums and is caused by the buildup of tartar on their teeth. If not properly treated, your dog is at risk of bacterial infections that could be lethal. The easiest way to avoid this is to brush your dog's teeth often. Every day if you have the time. This is an important part of puppy hygiene that people tend to overlook as it is time-consuming and difficult. In most cases, people will use a doggy toothbrush to do this, but if you are on a time crunch, veterinarians recommend just using your fingers to get the tartar out of your pup's teeth. I know it sounds gross but this is important to prevent bacterial infection. It is important to start training your dog when they are young to be comfortable with teeth brushing. This way there are less likely to develop gum disease and prevent bad behaviors like chewing on objects or other people.

*B*elow I will provide you with a set of directions to make the teeth brushing process a little easier and more comfortable for you and your canine friend.

1. Get a doggy toothbrush. There should be a wide variety of them at any pet store. Doggy toothbrushes have softer bristles that are made to give you easier access to the teeth that are harder to reach. Make sure to choose a toothbrush based on your dog's size. Obviously, bigger dogs will require a larger toothbrush, and smaller dogs will need a smaller one that can fit into their mouth. Like we mentioned earlier, using your finger to clean your dog's teeth is also a good option. There are products called finger brushes that fit onto the end of your finger which can give you better accuracy and precision during the brush. However, you may risk getting bit by your dog by using this technique. Avoid using human toothbrushes for your dog as the bristles are too hard and may damage your dog's mouth, tongue, or gums. If you aren't able to find a doggy

toothbrush, you can use a child's toothbrush with extra soft bristles.

2. Use doggy toothpaste. Just like toothbrushes, there is a variety of different doggy toothpaste at your local pet stores that are made specifically for dogs. Never use human toothpaste to brush your dog's teeth. Human toothpaste usually contains fluoride and other chemicals that are toxic to dogs. It is not harmful to us as we don't usually swallow our toothpaste, but many dogs will swallow toothpaste as their teeth are being brushed. Doggy toothpaste is also made in different flavors that your dog may enjoy to help make the process of brushing easier. Feel free to try different flavors to find one that best suits you and your puppy.

3. Get your dog comfortable with you having your hand in or near its mouth. When you first start brushing your dog's teeth, take it slow, and get your dog used to you being around its mouth area. When training your dog, get him/her used to you touching their muzzle area. It may take some time for your dog to get used to it but once they are, it is a lot less nerve-wracking for your dog.

4. Start the toothbrushing process by letting your dog lick and taste a small amount of the doggy toothpaste from your finger. This will help you understand how well your puppy likes the toothpaste. It will also help your dog get used to the taste of the toothpaste, which will make him/her more likely to be comfortable in the process.

5. Next, show the doggy toothbrush to your dog and let him/her sniff it and inspect it. Allow your dog to lick some of the toothpaste off the toothbrush. Make sure to praise your dog after this as it will positively reinforce this action.

6. In this step, begin to gently brush your pup's teeth. Start with the ones that are the easiest to reach. Their canine

teeth are the longest and the easiest to reach. Gently lift up your puppy's upper lip and brush their teeth gently back and forth. Do this gently and slowly to help your dog get used to the feeling of having a toothbrush on their teeth and gums. If your dog is reluctant or aggressive during the brushing, proceed with caution. To make it easier, have a friend or a family member help calm your pup as you brush their teeth. Remember to reward your dog after a few minutes of brushing and reward them again at the end.

7. Brush the outside of your dog's teeth. Once your dog has gotten used to the gentle brushing it is time to combine a few actions. Place some more toothpaste on your toothbrush and gradually brush along the entire outside surface of the upper and lower teeth. You can increase the number of teeth every time you brush. Make sure to brush along the gum line as well.

8. Once you have brushed all of your dog's teeth, make sure to brush the inside surfaces of your dog's teeth. Place one hand over the top of your dog's muzzle, lift their upper lips, and open his/her mouth. Once their mouth is open, start brushing the bottom of their upper teeth and the top of their lower teeth.

9. Make teeth brushing into a daily routine. The more often you brush your dog's teeth, the more he/she will get used to it. This will make teeth brushing easier over time.

Cleaning Your Dog/Puppy's Toys

If your dog's toys are going into their mouth repeatedly, it is important to make sure they are clean. However, don't clean your dog's toy with chemical sprays or disinfectants - that could be potentially poisonous to your dog. The best solution here is to soak your dog's chew toys in a water and vinegar solution for half an hour. Make sure to wash your dog's toys once a month to ensure safety.

Cleaning The Dog Bed

Most people don't know this, but one of the dirtiest things in your home is actually your dog's bed. A dog's bed is the ideal environment for fleas, germs, allergens, and ticks. Bathing your dog is useless if the bed they get into at the end of the night is dirty. To make your life easier, you can buy a dog bed that has a removable fabric cover that can be taken off and washed in your washing machine. If your dog is a breed that sheds often, you should vacuum your pup's bed at least once a week.

Cleaning Your Dog's Paws

Your dog's paws typically carry whatever they have stepped in. This includes things like pollens, pesticides, molds, pollutants, and dust mites. Since you shouldn't bathe your dog every day, it is important to clean their paws a couple of times a month. Clean it by soaking your dog's paw in warm water or just simply rub it down with a wet cloth. If you have a dog that is extra fluffy or hairy, make sure to trim the hair/fur between their toes and brush it as well. Helping your dog clean its paws will cut down on the amount that your dog chews and licks them.

Cleaning Your Doggy Accessories

For the inexperienced dog owners, you should know that after a while, your dog's collar will start to smell funky. Just like how it doesn't make sense to bathe your dog and then have him/her sleep in a dirty bed, it also doesn't make sense to put a dirty collar or harness on her. Although collars don't need to be washed often, as soon as you notice a smell or if it becomes black/brown - it is time for you to throw it in the washing machine. You can use pet-friendly detergent or simply just soak it in hot water with a little bit of doggy shampoo. This is an easy fix but an important one if you don't want a dirty and smelly dog collar.

When Do I Neuter/Spay My Dog?

If you are a first-time dog owner, you might be wondering if you need to spay/neuter your dog. The answer is 100% absolutely. Most dogs that you adopt from the shelter will already be neutered and spayed, but puppies won't be, so be sure you are planning ahead for this procedure. Not only will this prevent numerous medical issues for your dog, but it also helps reduce overpopulation which is a huge problem in many cities all over the world. Every year, millions of dogs are euthanized because shelters don't have the resources of space to care for that many animals. By making sure to neuter/spay your dog, you are playing your part to prevent this tragic problem.

*W*hat exactly is the difference between neutering and spaying? It's quite simple actually, male dogs get neutered, and female dogs get spayed. We will discuss the must-knows of each process below.

Spaying Your Female Dog

The spay surgery prevents female dogs from being able to get pregnant by removing the ovaries and uterus. It is otherwise known as getting your dog "fixed." This surgery is not as simple as the neuter surgery, it is a major surgery and your pup may be affected for up to a few weeks. However, she will enjoy numerous health benefits and you won't have to worry about her being in heat.

• • •

*S*ome dog owners think that they can easily prevent pregnancy just by keeping their dogs inside or in a secure yard away from male dogs. However, even experienced dog owners may have a surprise "oops"! Dogs can jump over or dig under gates to mate. When two dogs with raging hormones are near each other at the wrong time, you may have an accidental pregnancy.

*T*he main benefit of spaying your dog is to prevent unwanted pregnancies that may contribute to overpopulation. Like we mentioned earlier, millions of dogs are euthanized every year due to overpopulation in shelters. Besides this reason, there are several other benefits to spaying your dog.

- Getting your dog spayed reduces the risk of certain illnesses such as mammary gland cancer and pyometra (a common infection of the uterus that is life-threatening)
- Getting your dog spayed helps prevent males from being wildly attracted to your dog when in heat
- Getting your dog spayed prevents her from having her period, so you don't need to use sanitary pads or have a mess all over your home.
- Spaying eliminates a terrible odor that your dog releases when in heat. Although your nose is not as sensitive as a dog's, humans are still able to smell this distinct odor.

*F*emale dogs go into heat once every eight months or so and lasts up to three weeks at a time. They also don't go through menopause and will regularly be in heat for their entire lives until they are spayed. So when is the best time to spay your dog? A veterinarian will be able to make a recommendation based on your dog's breed and needs. Most female dogs have this surgery after 2 months and before their first heat (6 - 7 months). Some veterinarians will recommend spaying surgery right before the first heat so they could tolerate the necessary anesthesia. A larger and more fully grown dog is more difficult to spay than a smaller dog which is why veterinarians will give their recommendation on a case by case basis.

*J*ust like the neutering surgery, spaying surgery also requires pre-surgical blood work to make sure your pup is healthy enough for this big surgery. Young and healthy dogs typically won't have any issues but it is still a good idea to get blood work done. Although spaying is a common surgery, it is still a fairly major one. Your veterinarian will give you specific instructions for post-surgery care and your dog will likely fully recover after a few weeks. Here are a few things to expect after your dog has the surgery:

- Some clinics will let you take home your pup after the surgery on the same day, but other clinics may want her to stay overnight
- Pain medication will be prescribed on a need basis, most dogs don't need it, but some do.
- Your dog may have some nausea in the first couple of days

and may not be interested in food. This will go away after the first few days, so no need to worry.

- Restrict her activity and play in the first week as excessive movement and exercise can cause swelling around her incision.
- Depending on what type of stitches your veterinarian used, they may need to be removed after a week. Your veterinarian will give you directions on how to check on the healing process of your dog's incision. Some modern-day stitches dissolve or fall out on their own.
- Make sure to keep her "cone of shame" on to prevent licking or nibbling of her incision.

*I*f you notice any discharge around her incision, check in with your veterinarian to make sure everything is okay. Your dog shouldn't be in excessive pain, but if you notice that she is, let your veterinarian know as pain medication may be needed. Most dogs may feel lethargic and have low energy a few days after the surgery but don't worry. Give her a few days to recover before you get concerned.

Neutering Your Male Dog

Neutering is actually a very simple surgery that sterilizes a male dog so he cannot parent puppies. Neutering also lowers the risk of certain diseases, unwanted behaviors, and socialization problems. The neutering surgery is simpler than the spaying surgery. The veterinarian will put the dog under using anesthesia and make a small incision in the front of the dog's scrotum. The veterinarian will then cut the stalks of the testicle and then remove it through the incision. Most likely the incision will need stitches, and the dog will have to wear a 'cone collar' during its recovery to prevent licking or nibbling of the area. In just two short weeks, the incision would heal and the dog goes back to their normal life.

*B*esides not having the ability to conceive any puppies, there are many more reasons to neuter your dog. First of all, they are less likely to get diseases such as testicular cancer or prostate diseases. Due to having less testosterone in the dog's system, they will likely be calmer. In addition, dogs naturally mark their territory using their urine. Since they have less testosterone, your dog will naturally mark less. The lower level of testosterone should improve behaviors like aggression and humping. Although it is a myth that your dog will stop humping after being neutered, dogs still mount and hump to exert dominance and not solely just to mate. It is less likely that your dog will get into fewer fights with other male dogs.

*M*ale dogs can get neutered any time after two months of age. Veterinarians normally advise waiting until doggy puberty hits at six months, but it is a case by case scenario. Talk to your veterinarian to get the best recommendation for your specific dog breed. Dogs that get neutered before puberty (6 months) typically grow a bit bigger compared to those that are neutered after puberty because of the testosterone involved in bone growth. Depending on the owner, more growth may be more or less desirable. Keep in mind that most dogs are sexually mature by the fifth or sixth month so make the necessary preparations to have your dog neutered around that age.

· · ·

*T*he normal procedure of the neutering surgery starts with pre-surgical bloodwork for your dog. This is to make sure that your dog is healthy enough for surgery and doesn't have any preexisting conditions that may affect the anesthesia or surgery itself. More often than not, young dogs are healthy and won't have any issues, but it is still a step that is needed to get a reference for future bloodwork. Your dog should not eat for 8 hours before the surgery as the anesthesia may cause nausea.

*N*eutering surgery is typically very simple and straightforward. The harder part, however, is the post-surgery care for your dog. Here are a few things to keep in mind after your dog gets neutered:

- Male dogs/puppies usually are allowed to go home the same day after the surgery
- Your dog may have some nausea and not eat for a day or two. No need to worry as your dog will be fine if he misses a few meals. He will eat again once nausea fades.
- The first few days after the surgery, you may notice that your dog's scrotum is swollen. This is not harmful but just be sure that your dog cannot lick or irritate the incision. A lot of the times the swelling gets worse if your dog got access to the wound. By making your dog wear the "cone of shame," they will be unable to reach their scrotum area.
- Depending on what kind of stitches your veterinarian used, they may need to be removed after a week or two. Some will use self-dissolving stitches that will go away on its own.
- Try to restrict your dog's activity after the surgery if they

are playful. Try to make sure they are playing gently to prevent the incision from opening up.

- Some bruising may occur near the incision; this is normal.

*K*eep an eye out on your dog's incision to see if there is any discharge or if your dog is in excessive pain. It is rare for a dog to feel this much pain after this surgery, but it is possible. Contact your veterinarian if you see any unusual symptoms or behaviors in your dog. Your dog may not be his usual self right after the surgery but give him a few days to recover before you begin to worry.

Socializing Your Dog: Is This Important?

During your puppy's age of 2 to 4 months is the most important socialization period that shapes his/her future personality and how they will behave and react in their environment as an adult dog. By exposing them to different people, dogs, places, and situations make a huge difference in the future. If you are planning to purchase your puppy, make sure you do so from a responsible breeder. If your breeder is professional, the process of socialization is started earlier. Gentle handling by the dog's caretakers in the first few weeks of your pup's life is extremely helpful in developing a confident and friendly dog. Puppies at the early age of three weeks may begin to approach people who are watching them. Having a knowledgeable breeder encourages good future puppy behavior.

*S*o why is socializing your puppy necessary? Well, the idea of socialization is to get your puppy acclimated to the many different sounds, sights, and smells of the world in a positive manner. A properly socialized pup can prevent them from being scared or aggressive in certain situations.

*N*ow that you understand the importance of socialization, how do you do it? Begin by introducing him to new sounds, sights, and smells. To your brand new puppy, the entire world is new, unusual, and strange. Everything he/she encounters is an opportunity for you to make a positive association for him/her. Try to expose your puppy to as many different types of people, noises, places as you can to help your pup get used to it all. For example, expose him to different terrains such as pavement, grass, dirt, linoleum floors, hardwood floors, or carpets. It is important when you are exposing him to these different things that you are also making it a positive experience. Make sure you are giving him treats when he is positively reacting to certain things so your puppy can associate these new experiences with a reward. You can take the socialization one step further by involving your friends or family in the process. Continuously take your puppy out of his/her comfort zone and teach him that no matter who he/she is with that they will experience new things. Although there is a lot to expose your puppy to make sure you are taking baby steps. Avoid doing too much too quickly. For example, if you want your puppy to get used to different people, don't take him to a crowded park. Start by exposing him to a few people in a controlled environment and slowly integrate more people. Taking your puppy to a crowded public space may easily overwhelm him/her. Some dog owners may find it helpful to enroll their puppy in puppy school once they have all their vaccinations. Puppy school is a great way to socialize your puppy as they are exposed to other animals along with people.

Veterinarian Visits: How Often Do I Go?

A common mistake made by pet owners is only taking their dog to the veterinarian if he/she is feeling sick or if something happened. Make sure to keep up with routine visits as it is crucial to your pet's overall health. Routine visits help veterinarians assess how your dog is progressing through life and may help discover any underlying health conditions that your pet may have. A lot of the times, our dogs can have a serious issue that we aren't able to notice but a veterinarian would be able to pick these things up. The earlier you spot a problem, the easier it is to correct it or at least slow the condition down. During a general check-up, the veterinarian will perform a physical examination. This usually consists of a check that starts from your dog's nose all the way to their tail. They will inspect everything from the mouth, coat, paws, skin, and the tail. Checking your dog's dental health is an important part of the check-up as 80% of dogs are afflicted with dental problems. Bringing your dog to regular general check-ups will allow your veterinarian to make sure that your pup is caught up on his/her vaccines. Vaccinations are extremely important because they protect your dog against diseases that are fatal. Moreover, it also keeps other animals around you and your pup safe as well.

BENEFITS OF TRAINING YOUR DOG/PUPPY

A LOT of people are actually under the impression that you don't need to train your dog using a program. Simply just winging it good enough right? Nope. Without following specific techniques and a training program, it is very easy to confuse your dog, causing him/her to likely develop behaviors that you don't want. To avoid this, use a standardized training method and program that will be teaching you throughout this book to prevent that. Let's also take a look at some benefits of training your dog or puppy.

Benefit #1: Builds Stronger Relationships

Going through dog training with your buddy is the best way to building a closer bond. Based on a recent survey, dog owners who have a dog that is well-trained gain more satisfaction out of the companionship and has a stronger relationship with their pup. It means that if your dog is obedient, relaxed, happy, and well-behaved, that the two of you will get more pleasure out of the relationship. As a result, the owner will grow closer to their dog.

. . .

a lot of times, if a dog owner has not properly trained their dog, they may find themselves avoiding the dog due to the annoyance of their bad behavior. A common problem is that people will put their dog in a kennel or in a separate room and leave the dog alone for an extended period of time due to wanting to avoid bad behavior. Although this is effective in preventing your dog from damaging your home, it is extremely detrimental to your dog's health and your bond with them. The more a dog owner avoids their dog, the more separation anxiety the dog may feel. Separation anxiety is a common problem amongst household dogs. This can lead to even worse behaviors moving forward.

Benefit #2: Eases Management

Teaching your dog to learn basic commands like drop, sit, and stay will allow the owner ease of simple management. If your dog understands these commands, it means it is easy to manage your dog in most situations. For example, if your dog begins chewing on something he/she isn't supposed to be chewing on, you can command him/her to drop and sit. If your dog isn't properly trained and is uncontrollable, they tend to misbehave in other ways which then leads to being put away in a kennel or being left at home alone. By promoting better management by teaching their dogs commands, dog owners can prevent potential misbehavior. Teaching your dog simple things such as how to greet humans politely, walking on a lead in a controlled manner, and coming to you when you call them are all basic behaviors that owners desire and need. One thing that I will be emphasizing in this book is that it is much easier to prevent bad behavior than it is to teach good behavior. So instead of trying to fix bad behavior into good behavior, let's just start by preventing bad behavior from happening in the first place.

· · ·

*B*eing able to easily manage your dog also contributes to the overall safety of your dog. We've all heard of the occasional news story where somebody's dog broke off their leash and attacked a stranger. In these types of cases, it doesn't end well for the dog. Often, the court will order the dog to be euthanized as they will be deemed a threat to society. By making sure your dog learns the basic and most important commands can prevent a scenario like this from happening. Dogs that are obedient and well-behaved will not run away from you even if they aren't on a leash.

*A*nother thought you should keep in mind is choosing a breed of dog where the size of the dog is right for you. There are numerous cases where somebody who is of a smaller stature is trying to tame and control a large dog and is unable to do so. I don't recommend people owning large breeds of dogs (e.g., Mastiff or Great Dane) because of how difficult it is to control them physically while they are still being trained.

Benefit #3: Builds Positive Habits for Your Dog

Most people who spend a lot of time and effort training their dog tend to want their dog to be friendly and social. Just like we discussed in the previous chapter, socializing your dog is a very important aspect as it largely affects their adult behavior. You want your dog to get along with other animals and humans in the real world. To have a properly socialized dog, your dog must interact with other dogs and learn what is and isn't allowed in dog language. This is extremely important for dog owners who live in a big city. Chances are when you are out with your dog; you will likely come across another pet owner with their dog. Having a well-trained dog will prevent undesirable situations like growling, rough play, and aggressive barking.

Benefit #4: Safety

Ensuring that your dog is well trained is important for the safety of your family, especially if there are babies or young children around. One of the other main causes of dogs being given up to shelters is when a family has a newborn baby. Having a misbehaved dog in the circumstance of an infant is dangerous as the dog poses a big threat due to their unpredictability. Instead of having to give your dog up to the shelter if you have a growing family, train them so they are not a safety threat to babies and young children. If your dog is aggressive or is showing signs of aggression, get to the root cause of it instead of jumping directly to punishment. A lot of the time aggression comes from a deeper issue that could be health-related. In addition, there are cases where dogs become jealous if a new member of the family is introduced and they are receiving less attention than usual. Make sure to section out parts of your day where you can solely dedicate some time to bonding with your pup. They are sensitive beings too!

Benefit #5: Promotes a Healthy Community

Having a dog with good behavior is a great segue into meeting other dogs and dog owners within your community. When you are out and about with your trained pup, it is a strong indication that the two of you have a great bond. This is a great opportunity to start conversations with other dog owners in your community. Being able to connect with others and socialize will give you the opportunity to get involved in local dog events or activities. There are research and evidence that shows that people who own dogs are less prone to physical and psychological illnesses due to the extra exercise and socialization that they get. Often times, depending on the breed of your dog and its age, it can be very time consuming to properly train a dog. Some dog training professionals will advise new dog owners to take a few weeks off from work just to ensure that you are spending an adequate amount of time bonding and training your puppy. Although training is time consuming and requires a lot of effort, the benefits that come with it are huge. Rather than spending the next decade struggling with bad behavior from your dog, train your dog during their puppyhood so you can prevent a lot of future problems. Keep in mind the next time you and your pup are out in your community, take the time to meet other dog owners and share some tips and advice amongst each other. You may be pleasantly surprised that a lot of dog owners may be facing the same struggles as you and have found good solutions!

DIFFERENT TYPES OF DOG/PUPPY TRAINING

THIS CHAPTER WILL FOCUS on teaching you the different types of dog/puppy training out there. When dog training comes to mind, people typically think of the classic house training where your dog can do a few tricks, use the bathroom outside and stay off the furniture. However, there are actually many different types of training out there available to dogs. Depending on your needs, you have a variety of training programs you can choose from. For instance, emotional assistance dogs require a special type of vocational training in order to be granted a certificate that allows the owner and the dog special privileges in places that typically may not welcome dogs. In addition, you have probably seen seeing-eye dogs being trained in foster programs; this is a special type of dog training as well. I will teach you about the four most commonly used training programs; behavioral training, obedience training, agility training and vocational training. This will help you understand what type of training program you require for your dog.

Behavioral Training (House Training)

Behavioral training, or otherwise commonly known as house training, is the most basic and common type of training when it comes to canines. This training type is aimed to help your dog develop good etiquette in a person's home. Behavioral training aims to prevent undesirable behaviors in dogs which range from barking at guests to chewing up furniture or household objects. This simple form of training is absolutely necessary for every dog that lives in your home. This type of training is best applied when your dog is still a puppy, as that is when they are most impressionable. If you own multiple dogs, having one dog with bad behavior is enough to cause a domino effect with your other pups. Behavioral training is used for most dogs in order to alleviate some common behavioral problems that arise when the dog is not trained. Let's take a look at a few problems that behavioral training will help with:

- Jumping on people

The behavior of jumping on and at guests is also a common one when it comes to bad behaviors for dogs. This is normally due to excitement but can still be very annoying and shocking to the guest. Have you ever had a visitor over at your home and before you could say stop your dog has trampled them over? This is a popular problem. To prevent this situation, teaching your dog commands such as "sit" or "down" is extremely useful. Before you let your guests into your home, command your dog to sit and stay and have treats on hand to reward them if your dog remained sitting during the greeting. When your dog is in a seated position, they are unable to jump. Make sure to teach your guests to not give your dog any attention until they are acting calmly and in a seated position. Let your visitors know that if your dog jumps up at them any time during the greeting, to turn around and leave. This will let the dog know that their behaviors will drive people away.

- Jumping/sitting on furniture

Depending on your personal preference, you may or may not want your dog to be sitting on your couch with you or sleeping in your bed. This type of behavior needs training to be implemented from day one. Before you bring your dog home with you, decide whether or not you want your pup to be on the furniture with you. One mistake that dog owners make is to sometimes allow and sometimes not. This will confuse the dog as they won't know if it is a positive behavior or negative behavior. If you decide that you do not want your pup on your furniture with you, make sure you nudge them off any furniture they jump on to. Once they are off the furniture, give them a command such as "sit" or "down" and then reward with a treat once they are sitting calmly on the ground.

- Chewing on objects that aren't designated toys

During puppy development, chewing tends to be one of the bigger problems. During puppyhood, dogs go through 'teething.' This is when the puppy's baby teeth are being pushed out by the adult teeth that are growing. Usually, this happens when the puppy is around four months old. The act of their baby teeth being slowly pushed out can be irritating and painful for your dog. To soothe these feelings your dog may begin chewing on objects more often, some of which you probably don't want them sinking their teeth in. During the time of their teeth growth, provide a lot of chew safe toys for your puppy to play with. Chewing is very normal during this time period so instead of trying to prevent it, redirect your puppy's chewing to items that are meant to be chewed on. When you see your puppy chewing on their chew-toy, reward them with a treat. To keep things interesting, keep a stash of chew toys in your home and rotate new ones in and out to keep your dog entertained. If you have the time, try to go one step further and schedule in sessions of playtime for you and your dog. If your sessions are long and draining enough, your pup won't have the energy to chew on your favorite pair of shoes.

- Digging holes outside

Instinctually, dogs have a tendency to dig holes in the dirt to either bury and hide food or to make a cold spot to lie in during hot summers. Since this is a natural tendency, it is one of the harder behaviors to prevent. If you have space, set aside a small area in your yard where your dog is allowed to dog. Positively reinforce your dog to dig there instead of preventing it altogether. Direct your dog to the digging allowed area and reward them with a treat when they dig there. If your home does not have a digging area or a yard, you can distract your dog with toys or playtime so they don't have the time to dig. Things like frisbees or a game of fetch will usually redirect your dog's attention since it is way more fun. In addition, you should always be encouraging your dog to do physical activity as it prevents future health problems.

- Fear/anxiety

If your dog is properly socialized, it is not likely that they will be scared in most situations. If there are times where you notice your pup is fearful when they are put in a specific situation, be sure to consult your veterinarian. It can also be a sign of an underlying health issue especially if their behavior is not usually like this. When your dog is scared, they will likely refuse treats or attention so don't try to force a reward onto them. If your veterinarian determines that there are no health problems but are just scared in that specific situation, try accustoming your dog to that situation by making the experience as fun as possible. You can do this by encouraging play and giving them their favorite treat.

- Stealing food off counters/tables

The bad behavior of stealing food off of tables is actually an easier problem for humans to fix than dogs. You can simply prevent this behavior by not leaving food out on tables unattended when you know your dog is around. If there is no food left alone on table-tops, your dog won't even consider exploring that area because there is nothing of interest there. Be sure that you are not leaving food items that are dangerous to dogs out unattended. Grapes, chocolate, and alcohol are all items that are very toxic to dogs.

- Barking at people

Barking at guests or passersby of your home is a common problem in puppies. Have you ever taken a walk in your neighborhood, and when you walk past a certain home you hear aggressive barking from a dog? A lot of the times the barking may not actually be a sign of aggression but it is still extremely intimidating. Behavioral training can be used to redirect your dog's attention if they are in a barking spree. By teaching your dog commands such as "sit" and "stay" will direct their attention away from the people or guests outside and to the potential reward if they successfully do these actions. If you have visitors, you can use this technique by providing your guests with treats to give to your pup once they have calmly listened to the commands. By doing this every time you have guests, you will teach your dog to associate visitors and guests with polite behavior and a reward.

- Licking excessively

The act of licking excessively is a common behavioral problem in attention-hungry dogs. In the world of dog body language, licking is actually a sign of affection. You may think it is extremely cute and sweet for your dog to always be licking you, but it is not a good habit for them to develop unless you want to be covered in doggy slobber forever. To prevent this behavioral problem, don't give your dog any attention when they are licking you. In fact, stand up and walk away disinterested. When you notice that your dog has stopped licking you, reward them with a treat to let them know that not licking equals good behavior. Make sure to not give your dog any attention when they are licking you; otherwise, they will think that licking leads to attention.

- Running out doors/away from you

One of the more dangerous behavioral problems with dogs is running or pushing outdoors. If your dog is constantly dashing out of doors and into the street, it can be a terrifying experience. This is a dangerous habit as your dog may be harmed by traffic, cars, or other animals outside. To prevent behaviors like this, always train them to sit and stay before you open the door. Only when they are invited are they allowed to come outside with you. Reinforce this behavior by giving them a treat as a reward. Dog owners should always be teaching their dogs this as a safety precaution to prevent any accidents. If you are leaving your home without your dog, command them to sit and stay before you open the door. Give them a treat if they remain seated as you leave.

- Attention seeking

A lot of beginner dog owners fall into the trap of giving their dogs attention when they ask for it. A common behavior that puppies showcase is to bark, howl, or lick when they want attention. Even by telling your dog, "No!" or "Stop!" is still attention nonetheless to your dog. Instead of giving any time of reaction to your dog, ignore them and pretend that they aren't there. Certain dog breeds that are more attention-seeking like Huskies have the tendency to show attention-seeking behaviors. Once your pup settles down and is not asking for attention, you can then give them attention during that time to help them understand that only when they are not being demanding is when they will be praised and noticed.

- Aggression

If your dog is showing signs of aggression, the best thing to do is take them to a veterinarian to first eliminate any possible health problems. Aggression is not common amongst dogs and a lot of the times this behavioral problem is the result of an underlying health problem. Signs of dog aggression include things like biting, snapping, or lunging at other people and dogs.

- Meeting other dogs

One of the less commonly known facts about dogs is that they should never greet and meet new dogs while they are on a leash. This is because having a leash or harness on hinders your body language and will cause confusion between both parties. When there is confusion, it often leads to aggression from both sides. When your dog is still a pup, try to organize scheduled playdates with other dogs where they can freely greet each other without confusion. Dog parks are also a great place to go to meet other dogs since it is a leash-free zone. If you do come across another pup on a walk, command your pup to sit and stay before you introduce them to the other dog. Educate the other dog owner to do the same. Once they have successfully completed the action of staying seated during the initial greet, you may reward them with a treat.

Now that you have a good understanding of that behavioral training will help prevent, this is the minimum amount of training you should give your dog. Having this training will help your dog if you want to pursue other and more advanced types of training. Keep in mind that the most effective methods for dog training aren't to negatively reinforce bad behavior but to positively reinforce good behavior so your dog doesn't even think to do any behaviors that aren't positive. Bad behaviors are significantly more difficult to correct when your dog becomes an adult. By teaching your puppy good behaviors and habits from day one you will ensure that you guys have a happy and understanding companionship.

Obedience Training

Obedience training is meant to help dogs achieve complete obedience through the use of commands. This type of training is more advanced than the basic behavioral training as you will need your dog to have good behaviors already before you can begin obedience training. The difference between behavioral training and obedience training is that you are able to use commands without a particular reason to do so. For example, during behavioral training, if your dog tends to dash out the door when it is open, you will give them the command "sit" and "stay" before you open the door to prevent the running from happening. However, in obedience training you train your dog will listen and obey your commands regardless of the situation.

Obedience training commands range from simple 'must-know' commands all the way to competition level where dogs are scored and ranked for their performance and accuracy. A lot of the time, obedience training also utilizes hand gestures and body language to communicate the command to your dog. The dogs that you see in dog shows, competitions, or movies have definitely gone through intense obedience training. Trust between the human and the dog is the main key to success for obedience training.

In the beginning stages of obedience training, you will teach your dog these simple must know commands:

- "Sit": This command is used to direct your dog into a sitting position.
- "Down": This command is used to direct your dog into laying down. Their front feet and legs should be touching the ground.
- "Stay": This command is used to direct your dog to remain in the same position on where you used that command.
- "Come": This command is used to call your dog over to you.
- "Heel": This command is normally used during walks where you direct your dog to keep their head parallel to your legs.
- "Drop it" or "leave it": This command is used to direct your dog to drop whatever is in his/her mouth or to stay away from an object that they are approaching.

There are more difficult commands that can be taught once your puppy has completed the necessary behavioral training. For simplicity's sake, we will only be using these commands during your puppy's training period. In the next book, where we focus on training for adult dogs, we will dive more in-depth regarding more advanced commands that can be taught to your companion.

Agility Training

Agility training is a very unique type of training that is drastically different from obedience training/behavioral training and vocational training. It is only normally used for dogs and owners that want to participate in competitions or dog shows. Agility training includes activities like obstacle courses, racing and jumping. If you have seen a dog show before and witnessed the doggy competitors doing amazing physical stunts, then it is safe to say that they have all gone through agility training. A big difference between agility training and obedience training is that the dog owner/handler is not allowed to reward, praise, or touch their pooch during a competition or show. The pair will need to have a very strong bond and connection through the use of body language and vocal commands. Technically every single breed of dog has the ability to learn agility training but certain breeds of dogs are naturals at it.

Agility training is an advanced level of dog training and is only recommended to the owners who have the necessary time and resources. If you are someone that is looking to get more involved in the dog competition/show community, this is a great way for you and your pooch to get participating. In addition, agility training is also a type of training that is commonly used as a solution for dogs with high energy levels. If you have a breed of dog that requires a lot of exercise, this is a fun way for you and your buddy to get some exercise. Plus, if you guys win some competitions you can even get some cash prizes! If you are interested in agility training, it actually brings a ton of benefits to you and your dog.

First of all, agility training helps fulfill a dog's natural instinct. Agility training can help with dogs that have a ton of energy that could turn into bad behavior if not properly managed. Since dogs used to be wild, they were not always domesticated. Back in their wild days, dogs were natural hunters and scavengers. They constantly did daily tasks such as chasing and hunting prey in the wild. On an average day, dogs had to maneuver through lots of natural obstacles. This can range from running through forests whilst dodging trees all the way to climbing up steep slopes and mountains. To be able to catch a satisfying meal, a wild dog would need to run very fast to catch their prey. The faster they were, the higher the chance of them being able to eat dinner that night. In the present day, agility courses mimic the natural terrain and obstacles to help your dog to satisfy their natural desire to hunt.

Secondly, agility training provides your dog with a ton of exercise. This is especially good if you have a breed of dog that naturally has a lot of energy and need for running around (like a border collie). If you are one of those owners who has a dog that is extremely high energy, agility training can be the perfect solution for you. Most veterinarians and dog training professionals do not recommend owning dogs as pets if you live in a small space. Like we just mentioned, it is in a dog's instinct to run around and dodge obstacles. Living in a confined space for a dog is not ideal because they don't have the room to move around or get the exercise they need. If you are someone who lives with their dog in a smaller space, agility training may be a good solution for the two of you. Dogs that participate in agility training typically spend lots of time doing obstacle courses that are made up of crawls, jumps, and tunnels. This is a great way to challenge your pooch's body and mind. According to recent research, dogs that participate in agility training are proven to have stronger muscles and better physical health. They also have improved coordination and endurance compared to dogs who don't do agility training. If you find that your dog is being destructive due to lack of exercise, it may be time to sign up for some agility training courses.

In addition, if you are someone that's lacking some serious exercise, agility training will help you get fit as well! Since agility training requires the pooch and the human to participate together, you will be able to get some good exercise as well! Unlike dogs, people oftentimes have trouble getting the motivation to do physical activity. This is a great way for you to get your juices flowing while you are agility training your pup! During this type of training, the dog owner has to be constantly running next to their dog and helping guide them over jumps, weave around poles, and crawling through tunnels. You'd probably find that at the end of the training session that you are more out of breath than your dog!

Agility training is also a great way to strengthen the bond between you and your pup. There are many aspects of an obstacle course where it requires the full trust of the dog and human for your dog to be able to complete it. The dog actually relies heavily on the commands that are given by the owner to be able to navigate through the obstacles properly. Due to the mutually beneficial relationship, trust between you and your dog will naturally grow. Recent research has proven that the act of doing obstacle courses with your dog through agility training improves your dog's home behavior and reinforces the basic obedience and behavioral commands. If you have the opportunity, go and watch a dog show in your free time. Make sure to pay attention to the dog handlers and the dogs themselves. You will notice that some of the dogs in these shows are the most well-behaved dogs. Agility training can help you achieve a healthy and obedient companion.

Vocational Training

When it comes to dog and puppy training, vocational training is the most advanced type. This type of training is so advanced to the point that the dog has to pass multiple healthy, intelligence, and obedience exams before they can even qualify to participate in any kind of vocational training. The most common vocational dogs we see in our daily lives are sightseeing dogs or police dogs. The dogs you see with jobs have gone through the most advanced level of training and are incredibly intelligent and obedient. For example, search and rescue, hunting, policing, and assisting the disabled are all jobs that dogs can do with vocational training. This type of training cannot be conducted by your average dog owner. You have to enroll your dog into special programs where dogs are taught very specific techniques that utilize their five senses to communicate with humans effectively. The programs that offer this training are usually very time consuming and rigorous. All dogs need to have an incredible foundation of basic obedience skills before they can enroll in vocational training. Similar to agility training, there are specific breeds of dogs that are better suited for this advanced-level program.

If you are interested in helping your puppy go through vocational training one day, we will be discussing a few types of jobs that dogs with this training can do and what specific requirements are needed. Keep in mind that vocational training is extremely advanced and should not be attempted by anyone other than a professional. If you try this at home with your dog you may end up causing your dog more confusion and may actually backtrack some of their existing training progress.

The first and most common type of vocational training is for service dogs. Service dogs are probably the most common dogs with jobs that we see in our daily lives. Service dogs are trained to help people with disabilities. This can include people who are visually impaired, or people with physical disabilities. There are even more specialized service dogs that help those who are hearing impaired or suffers from seizures. A service dog that is fully certified is extremely well behaved in every type of situation and public areas. This type of dog is so well socialized that they are able to accompany their humans everywhere they go. A lot of people confused service dogs with therapy/emotional support dogs, but they are entirely different! Golden Retrievers, Labradors, Poodles, and German Shepherds are typically the breeds that are selected for vocational training due to their natural qualities. They often are more obedient by nature and therefore naturally better at this type of training. This is why you hardly ever see a french bulldog as a working dog!

The second type of vocational training is for emotional support dogs or therapy dogs. These dogs are trained to be a component of somebody's medical therapeutic program. Therapy dogs main purpose is to offer emotional support to people that are injured or suffering from an illness. They can either live with the person in their home and offer support 24/7, or they pay visits to places like a hospital or a nursing home. Therapy dogs commonly visit schools and daycares to help educate children about what working dogs actually do. One of the main differences between service dogs and therapy dogs is that therapy dogs can be any breed of dog as long as they have the proper training, temperament, and socialization. The only qualification to become a therapy dog is to have an even-temper. Moreover, therapy dogs can receive training from anyone and not only professionals. As long as they can pass the examination, they can be certified!

The next type of vocational training that is offered is training for police dogs. When you think about police dogs, your mind probably automatically wanders to action movies. Police dogs are often called 'K-9s'. Their main purpose is to aid law enforcement professionals such as the police. K-9s main purpose is to protect their handlers and help chase down fleeing criminals. Often times, police dogs are also trained to sniff out illegal substances at large events (e.g., a concert) or at the airport. Although K-9s can typically do their job of protecting and sniffing, there is an entire unit of 'detection dogs' where they focus only on sniffing out illegal substances. The German Shepherd is the chosen breed for this type of work due to their extremely sensitive noses and wolf-like stature that gives them the advantage of speed when in a criminal chase.

The last type of vocational training is similar to police dogs but are for military dogs. Military dogs assist the military force rather than the police force. They are normally utilized during military missions where the dogs perform tasks like tracking, search and rescue, scouts, and detectors. It is pretty rare to come across a military dog as they usually live in army bases. Again, the most common breed of dogs used for this job is German Shepherds. Other breeds are utilized as well such as the Belgian Malinois and Dutch Shepherds. These three breeds share similar wolf-like traits which give them the advantage of incredible running and detection skills.

With this new information, you can now decide for yourself if you would like to pursue any of these advanced levels of training for your dog. Keep in mind that before you can enroll your dog in these programs that they must have some sort of obedience or behavioral training first. If you simply just want to have a companion that is well-behaved, none of this training is necessary. However, if you are interested in helping out the service dog community, there are likely local resources you could look into. Most of the times, every city has a guide dog program where they accept volunteers to foster guide dog puppies and give them the basic behavioral training and obedience training so they can qualify for the training program. If you want to take your dog training skills and knowledge one step further, this might be a good program for you to participate in.

UNDERSTANDING DOG/PUPPY BEHAVIORS

As I mentioned in this book, understanding dog/puppy behavior is just as important as the actual training itself. This will help you get an idea of what your dog is trying to tell you and will help you identify what is a behavioral issue or if your dog is suffering from health issues. Since dogs cannot speak to us, many dog owners struggle with understanding what their dog is trying to tell them. I will be teaching you about many different types of dog behaviors and explain to you what they mean. Certain distinctive behaviors can mean a serious health problem while other behaviors may simply be your dog acting up. Let's take a look at the list below:

1. Biting

Dogs use biting as their instinctual way to communicate with their mothers. Puppies tend to nip at their human owners when they are trying to communicate before they learn a better communication method. Dogs often use their mouths to interact with humans. It is really important in puppy training to stop biting behavior before it develops into a habit. Especially if you have a larger breed of dog, if your dog is constantly biting it can be a problem when they are fully grown.

Besides communication, biting is usually caused by aggression, anxiety, or fear. The first step is to try to figure out what is motivating your puppy to bite. It could be because they are looking to play, looking for attention, or looking to soothe irritation in their mouth. If you don't think that your puppy is biting for those mentioned reasons, consider consulting your veterinarian cause the issue may run deeper than what we see on the surface. Getting to the bottom of it will help ensure a healthier relationship with you and your pup.

Here are a few tips to help control and prevent your dog from biting. An effective technique is called 'Bite Inhibition,' this method teaches your puppy to be more gentle. Instead of getting rid of biting all together, this technique aims to teach your puppy to control the intensity and force of their bite. By teaching your puppy that humans have sensitive skin, they will learn to control their bite; otherwise, they may hurt their owner. Between puppy to puppy, they learn bite inhibition naturally when they are playing together. A puppy may bite another puppy too hard and the puppy will yelp and stop the play altogether. The puppy who did the biting will likely be surprised by the yelp and pause the playing. This type of interaction teaches puppies to control their biting strength so they don't hurt one another because hurt equals no more play!

Human and puppy playtime is very similar when learning bite inhibition. Play with your puppy normally until he/she bites you too hard. When that happens, immediately yelp in a high-pitched manner, act as if you are very hurt, and let your arm/hand go limp. This will surprise your puppy and cause the play to stop, and for him/her to stop biting. If he stops biting, give him praise, and continue playtime. If he/she does not stop the biting, then immediately stop playing and give him a time out. Yelp every time your puppy tries to bite you and ignore him/her for at least 30 seconds after every painful bite. If he still does not stop biting or begins to bite in a more gentle manner, get up and move somewhere else for another 30 seconds. After that, you can continue playing with your puppy but make sure to stop immediately if hard biting continues. By repeating this pattern, you will encourage your puppy to play gently but discourage hard biting by ending playtime.

1. Digging

We mentioned this briefly in the earlier chapters about how digging is a natural instinct for dogs. Dogs normally dog to either hide food, track animals, escape, or just make a cool spot in the dirt to lie in during a hot summer day. However, there are cases where dogs try to dig when they are inside. Some people have caught their dog digging into the bed or couch just to find a good spot to lie in. Normally this behavior is seen at night and is actually not a sign of an underlying medical condition.

If your dog's digging is starting to negatively affect you or the people around you, you can follow these techniques. Make sure to be walking and exercising your dog every single day. The most common reason for behavioral problems in dogs is actually the lack of exercise. When your dog begins to dig, try to tempt them to do something more fun like a game of tug of war or fetch. If your dog has good obedience training, you can get them to stop digging by giving them a command and rewarding them after.

If your dog still doesn't stop digging, they may actually be doing it to entertain themselves or to get your attention. If you think that your dog is doing it for entertainment, try to avoid leaving your dog outside in the yard by themselves for an extended period of time. Your dog will likely be bored out there by themselves and turn to the only entertainment they have, which is digging. A rule of thumb is to actually fill your home with dog toys so your dog always has something to play with. Make sure to always have a few of their favorite toys lying around so they can entertain themselves when you are not around. In addition, if your dog's breed is a Terrier, they are actually natural diggers. If this is the case, it would be a good idea for you to set aside a small space in your yard where your pup can act out their natural instincts.

If your dog is a chronic digger, make sure you curb the habit right away before it becomes a long term issue. When in doubt, always give your dog as much exercise as you can as this typically will solve most behavioral problems. Get into the habit of taking your dog out to the dog park to play with others. Playing with other dogs will save you the energy of having to run around, and they will also be distracted by other things and be too busy to dig. By involving your pup with other dogs at the dog park is a great way for your pup to burn off their incredible amounts of energy.

1. Head pressing

Head pressing is when a dog is pressing its head area against the wall or on other firm objects. If you see this happening, you need to give it immediate attention. Usually, this is a sign for numerous serious problems such as toxic poisoning or brain disease. If you see this happening, immediately take your dog to the veterinarian to figure out what the problem is. Possible medical conditions include; tumor growth, metabolic disorder, head trauma or a nervous system infection.

This is one of those behaviors that I advise dog owners to remember and to actively look out for. The earlier you can identify the issue and get help, the higher the likelihood of your dog being diagnosed and helped. This is commonly mistaken for a weird quirk that a dog may have, but it is actually quite the opposite.

1. Sitting on your legs/feet

If your dog is often trying to sit right on your legs or in between your feet, it is a sign of nervousness and anxiety. A lot of the times this is mistaken for dominance, but that is definitely not the case.

To mitigate this behavior, try to create a less anxious environment for your dog. Things like leaving your dog isolated in a confined space is extremely anxiety-inducing. Instead of banishing your dog to a confined area to avoid any accidents, allow your dog to roam your home while you are away but make sure you have given them the proper behavioral or house training. When a dog is sitting at your feet or right on you, they are showing that they are afraid of being left behind or being separated from you. This type of behavior occurs in dogs that live in families who move around a lot. If you are someone who is constantly moving, you may want to consider staying in a permanent place instead. Family members or roommates that are always coming and going maybe a source of anxiety for your dog as well. They may be afraid that everyone will leave and never come back at some point. Keep these reasons in mind if you notice this behavior in your dog so you can start trying out a few solutions that we mentioned.

1. Urinating in inappropriate places

If you haven't house trained your dog yet, it may not come as a surprise to you if you catch your pup urinating inside your home. However, if they have been house trained and normally do their business outside and they are suddenly urinating inside your home, then there may be a deeper-rooted issue. If your dog suddenly begins to urinate inside this may require your immediate attention. It could likely be due to an illness such as; urinary tract infection, bladder infection, or a kidney infection. If your dog happens to be old in age, then it could possibly be a symptom of dementia.

If you have confirmed that the urinating is not a health issue, then it is likely a behavioral issue. In the scenario that your dog is potty trained properly and is reverting back to this bad behavior, your dog could be doing it in response to a new situation. It could possibly be that you have introduced a new pet in the home, or a new child, or are you having strangers over to get some renovations done? All of these above scenarios are confusing to dogs and could easily cause distress. In some cases, it could even be something very insignificant like purchasing a new rug, and your dog instinctually wants to mark it by urinating on it.

Luckily, there are a few solutions to tackling this problem. The first is to be extra diligent in watching your dog for signs of urinating. Every dog will showcase obvious signs like lifting up one leg, sniffing, or circling. As soon as you see this, alert your dog by making a loud noise and take them outside to pee. Reward and praise if they successfully urinated outside. Although sometimes this method may be messy, it is the most straightforward way to teach your dog that peeing outside is good, and peeing inside is bad. The second solution would be to remove any smell or scent of previous accidents in your home. Usually, dogs will go back to the same spots that they have peed in instinctually. By making sure you are getting rid of all existing smells, it will be less likely for your dog to pee in the same spot again. Keep in mind to only use products that are made to remove pet urination scents. Simple wiping it down with water or soap won't actually get rid of the scent. The last method that you could use is to try the water spray method. This is a common technique where you spray your dog with water when they are doing an undesirable behavior. It is not harmful but is shocking enough to make them stop whatever they are doing. Simply when you catch your dog about to urinate inside, spray them with the bottle, then take them outside quickly. If they are successful in urinating outside, reward with a treat and praise. Keep in mind that punishment is proven to be an ineffective technique when it comes to training puppies and dogs. Avoid using any harsh punishment and instead praise good behavior.

1. Bad breath

Technically bad breath isn't a behavior, but it is still something that affects both you and your dog. Have you ever come across a dog that has breath so bad that you need to hold your nose? A lot of the times if your dog has bad breath, it is a sign that there could be something wrong with their oral hygiene and health. Remember that you ideally should be brushing your dog's teeth every single day. Instead of using band-aid fixes like feeding your dog doggy mints to mask the smell, it is a good idea to take your dog to the veterinarian to make sure everything health-related is okay. If you notice that your dog's breath smells different lately, it can have something to do with his kidneys, gastrointestinal tract, teeth, or liver. If you notice that your dog's breath smells sweet, it can be a sign of diabetes. If your dog's breath kind of smells like urine, it could be a kidney problem. These are small details that dog owners should be paying attention to as it could mean the difference between life and death.

1. Circling

If your dog is constantly walking around in circles and not the usual tail chasing, it could just be a weird quirk, but there may be an underlying health problem. A lot of the times, ear infections are a common reason behind a dog's circling habit. If you notice that your dog is not only just chasing their tail, but circling compulsively - it may be a good idea to take them for a check-up. If your veterinarian concludes that it is not a health problem, then it is likely a behavioral issue.

One of the early signs of compulsive disorders within dogs is circling. If this is not treated and ignored, the circling and spinning may become worse and harder to fix. The first step into tackling this issue is to keep a close eye on your dog. When you notice that your dog begins to spin or circle, immediately shake something to make a lot of noise (e.g., a jar of coins or a lanyard of keys). The noise should immediately distract your dog and stop him/her from spinning temporarily. Next, offer your dog a toy and if he/she becomes interested, encourage him/her to play with the toy instead. If your dog succeeds at this, reward him by offering a treat. If you have roommates or family living with you and you aren't able to use noise to distract your dog, try giving him a command like "sit" or "down" when you catch your pup spinning. Again, reward your dog with a treat when the command is fulfilled. Do this every single time you catch your dog circling or spinning.

Another method to solve a dog's spinning problem is to try to lower their energy levels as much as you can. Just like a human, take them out for an intense exercise session. In this scenario, you may even want to consider agility training if your dog has a bad habit of circling. Exercise is incredibly relaxing for dogs and the more calm and relaxed your pup is, the less likely it is for him/her to start circling. If you can squeeze in at least 30 minutes of exercise a day with your dog, it should start to help with the circling and spinning problem.

If you are unable to take extra time out of your day to exercise your dog, try to give your dog different kinds of entertainment at home. Boredom is a likely cause of spinning, so preventing problems may solve the circling issue. However, avoid entertaining your dog with things like a laser pointer as that tends to make spinning/circling habits worse. Try to entice your dog with food-stuffed chew toys instead. In addition, make sure you are not confining your dog in a small space like a kennel or a cramped room. Circling habits can actually be triggered by confinement over long amounts of time. Remember that dogs are naturally very athletic animals and require a ton of exercise every day. If you are someone who is planning or already keeping your dog in a crate or kennel every day, you might want to choose another method to contain them. If possible, hire a dog walker that can help exercise your dog during the hours that you are away from home.

1. Eating other dog's poop or their own poop

If you've never owned a dog before, the concept of your dog eating poop may be extremely foreign to you. However, most dog owners know that dogs often eat poop they find in public places, or even worse - their own poop. Although the thought of this is super gross to us, it is actually fairly normal behavior in the dog world. Baby puppies watch their mothers clean them with their mouth and ingest their feces. Your dog may actually be trying to copy the natural instincts of their mother. There are multiple reasons why a dog would eat its own poop. It can simply be just out of curiosity, or it could be eating their own poop because he/she pooped in an inappropriate spot and is trying to hide it.

If your dog is a serial poop eater, it is important to find out what the reason is. According to scientific studies, the main reason for a dog eating its own poop is due to isolation or restrictive confinement. If dogs are forced to stay in a restrictive space like a cage or a kennel, they are more likely to eat poop compared to dogs that have a larger area to roam and exercise. Often, anxiety is the reason behind a dog eating their own poop. Avoid using harsh punishment with your dog as this may actually cause them to eat more poop to avoid repercussions. Another reason behind poop eating is to seek attention. It is likely that your dog is eating its poop in order to get your attention. If you think this is the case with your pup, don't have a big reaction if you catch your dog in the act.

There are a few solutions you can use to avoid this gross behavior. First, try not to use products like "pee pads" or "puppy pads" for your dog to use indoors. These products allow your dog to leave their poop out without any supervision which may be giving your dog the opportunity to eat their own poop. Instead, house training your dog by teaching them to use the bathroom outside. Once they finish their business, pick up after them immediately so they don't have the chance to eat it. If they don't have the chance to eat their own poop, they won't be given the opportunity to develop this bad habit. If you also have a cat in your home, you may discover that your dog may be eating from your kitty's litter box! You can prevent this by simply placing the litter box somewhere that only the cat can get to. You may want to build or purchase an enclosed litter box where only your cat can get into. The only thing worse than your dog eating its own poop is eating your cat's poop!

1. Panting

Unlike humans, dogs don't sweat, but instead, they expel body heat through their mouth. If your dog is constantly panting, there is a high possibility that they are too warm and are trying to cool off in order to regulate their body temperature. However, you should still keep an eye out for excessive panting as it could also be due to pain. If you notice that your pup is panting heavily, help him/her cool off by offering water. If the panting still does not stop after that, it could be likely due to pain. Give your dog a quick look over and check to see if they have any signs of injury. You may want to consult your veterinarian just in case.

If you've concluded that your dog's panting is not due to pain or the heat, then it may be a symptom of anxiety. A lot of dogs share a common anxiety of loud noises, such as thunderstorms. If your dog is panting due to their fear of a specific situation, remember to stay calm. Dogs are able to feel people's anxiety so if you are panicking, he/she may get even more anxious. Try to encourage your dog to relax but avoid distracting him with things like treats or toys as this may actually create more stress. Try a few methods like wrapping your dog in a blanket or a jacket to help him feel safer. Obviously, if you can leave a specific situation that is anxiety-inducing for your dog, do so. Be there for your dog by comforting him and speaking softly and encouragingly.

1. Scooting

If you have ever seen your dog dragging their butt across your living room floor, it's quite a sight to see! However, it is often by the poop streaks on the floor. This behavior is called scooting, and it usually means that your dog feels some sort of irritation in their butt area.

A common reason for this irritation is due to your dog's anal sacs needing to be excreted. In addition, allergies are also a common cause of an itchy butt. A common myth is that worms are the cause of a dog's scooting but that is not true at all. The first step is to always check in with your veterinarian to make sure this is not a symptom of an underlying health problem.

If you've confirmed with your veterinarian that this is not due to a health problem, then it is likely that your dog likes to eat grass or likes to lick your floors. Eating grass or licking floors can cause your dog to consume strands of hair or blades of grass. Eating these things will lead to poop being stuck or 'dangling' around your dog's butt as they are trying to defecate. This annoying sensation is the reason why they begin to start scooting on the floor to get rid of the dangling poop. You can prevent this by not letting your dog eat grass when outside and to make sure that there aren't any stray hairs on the floors of your home. If your dog has the basic obedience training, you can also prevent them from eating objects like that by commanding him/her to "drop it" or "leave it."

1. Yawning

Yawning is one of those dog behaviors that humans don't give much attention to. A lot of the times people mistaken yawning as their dog is sleepy, or tired. Contrary to common belief, yawning doesn't always mean that your pup is just tired or sleepy. If you notice that your dog is yawning a lot, it is actually symptoms of fear or stress. If you catch your dog yawning around a new animal or person, be careful with how you introduce them. It is very likely that your dog is uncomfortable with these new people/animals or is scared for other reasons. Forcing introductions are never a good idea because it can cause future anxiety problems.

When it comes to dog body language, yawning is actually a calming action for them. Your dog is trying to tell you that they are getting impatient and that they are fed up. Some people may find that their dog begins to yawn during longer training sessions. This doesn't mean they are tired, but more so means they are frustrated and need a break. If you catch your dog yawning during a training session, try changing your approach or lowering the intensity of it.

Do keep in mind that sometimes a yawn really is just a yawn. If your dog or puppy has done some intense exercise or its getting late in the evening, it may simply be a normal yawn. Pay attention to the amount that your dog is yawning and make your own judgment on if it is appropriate given the circumstances.

DOG TRAINING TECHNIQUES

WITH YOUR NEW knowledge of dog behaviors, dog training types and stages of dog growth, you are not ready to learn about the various dog training techniques. Here, you will be introduced to five different techniques that can be used to train your dog; the alpha dog technique, positive reinforcement, clicker training, mirror training, scientific training and relationship-based training. The most commonly used type of training is positive reinforcement seconded with clicker training. You will see these training techniques used as the primary techniques in most puppy schools or used by professional dog trainers. Techniques such as mirror training and scientific training are used by professionals that do a lot of study and research in the field of dog training. Let's start learning about these techniques.

Positive Reinforcement

The first technique we will be looking at is the positive reinforcement technique. This technique is the most commonly used dog training technique and arguably the most effective one on the market right now. The theory behind the positive reinforcement technique is very simple. They follow the rule of dogs will repeat good behavior when it is rewarded. Bad behavior does not stipulate a reward or any acknowledgment at all. There is no harsh punishment used in this technique, but instead, punishment will be in the form of no rewards or praise. This technique strictly follows the theory that harsh reprimands are ineffective in training dogs.

*T*he way that positive reinforcement works is by rewarding your dog every time they do a good behavior like obeying a command, or simply doing something good without your direction. Once they complete that good behavior, you will reward your dog with a second of that action so your dog is able to associate the reward with that specific action. A lot of the times this training is paired with clicker training to help the dog understand when exactly their action was completed. The commands that you are using in this training should be very short like "sit" or "stay." Avoid using long terms like "Can you sit?" or "Please sit down." If you are using positive reinforcement, I would advise you to invest in a portable treat bag that you can carry around with you at all times. This way, when you catch your dog doing good behavior, you can present them with a reward right away. If you are taking too long to give the reward after the desired action, your dog may associate a different behavior to the reward instead. I would even advise new dog owners to give the reward just before the dog has completed the action in order to avoid a wrong association.

*T*he most important component of positive reinforcement is consistency. Although your dog may have learned all the behaviors you want and actions, it doesn't mean that you can stop practicing. Dogs will forget certain behaviors and action later on in life if it is not properly reinforced often enough. In addition, make sure that you are consistent with the training by educating other people you live with to do the same actions as well. This will help your dog learn the behavior of listening to other people instead of only listening to you.

*O*nce your dog has fully learned a command or behavior, you can gradually switch over to intermittent rewards. This way, your training is not solely relying on food, and you can use verbal praise and other ways to reward your dog. Make sure that you are not using rewards to lure your dog away when they are exhibiting bad behavior. A lot of new trainers will offer their dog a treat to get them to stop barking or jumping. This is incorrect as it will teach your dog that barking and jumping warrants a reward. Instead, if your dog is exhibiting bad behaviors, simply give them a command like "down" or "sit" and once they have quietly completed that task, give them a reward. Never ever reward your dog when he/she is exhibiting bad behavior or you will have a big problem in your hands!

*A*lways remember that only good behaviors will be rewarded. Rewards don't necessarily always have to be in the form of food, but it could be in the form of toys, praise, and pets. Be sure that you are not overfeeding your dog, especially if they are an adult or senior. Make sure your treats are healthy and in small sizes, so your dog doesn't put on weight. Once your dog has learned a behavior or command very well, you can switch over to intermittent rewards for that specific action and start rewarding when your dog has learned a completely new behavior. Again, be very disciplined in keeping an eye out of your dog's behavior and be ready to reward when they exhibit something desirable.

Alpha Dog Technique

The second technique we will be looking at is the alpha dog technique. This technique is based on the pack-mentality of dogs and utilizes the natural hierarchy of dogs to help implement desired behaviors. The theory behind this technique is that dogs will naturally follow their Alpha. Often times, our domestic pet dog sees themselves as an Alpha, which leads to behavioral problems like aggression or spraying. Our dogs will need to see us as the Alpha instead and show respect. You need to have a good knowledge of your dog's body language and communication to properly respond to your dog while projecting authority and confidence.

*I*f you decide that this is the method you are choosing to train your dog with, you need to set a few rules. First of all, your dog is not allowed to sit or sleep with you on furniture. You should never kneel down to meet your dog's eye level. These are all signs in the world of dog body language that you are equals. Keep in mind that you need to also follow the rules of the dog hierarchy system if you want your dog to see you as the Alpha.

*A*s the Alpha, you are the leader of the pack and you always come first. If you live with other people, they are also Alphas and they need to be involved in this training technique. Alphas are always the first to eat, leave, and sit. You have to make sure that you are commanding your dog to "sit" or "down" if you notice him/her trying to do those tasks before you. For example, if your dog wants to go outside for a walk, you have to command him to "sit" and "stay" before you open the door and let him/her out. You have to make your dog work for the things he/she wants.

. . .

*Y*ou have now learned the three most common and effective training techniques. The next few techniques that you will learn are less common and not as highly recommended as the above. However, if you feel like your dog is more suited for one of these techniques, you can go ahead and implement them.

Clicker Training

Clicker training is a popular technique that is typically used alongside with positive reinforcement training. It relies on the same fundamentals of positive reinforcement training but incorporates the use of a clicker. A clicker is a device that makes a two-toned clicking noise that is loud but brief. The purpose of the noise is to let your dog know that they have accomplished the desired behavior or action.

*T*he advantage of incorporating a clicker into training is its ability to let your dog know the exact moment that he has completed a task. Once you have clicked, you are able to follow up with a reward. A lot of people struggle with the timing of positive reinforcement and complain that their dog isn't able to learn the desired behavior. This way, your dog knows exactly when an action has been completed and will be expecting a reward as they hear the click. Some professional dog trainers consider positive reinforcement and clicker training the same type of training.

*C*licker training is most effective when you are using it to teach your dog new commands and behaviors. This is particularly effective with adult dogs that may have come from a different home, and you want to teach him/her commands specific to your needs. Clicker training is also extremely helpful in helping shape tasks that your dog is already familiar with into more complicated ones. This technique is great for learning new commands and behaviors but does not contribute much to curbing unwanted behaviors.

*B*elow are a set of instructions and tips on how you can use clicker training to train your dog. This technique is best suited for puppies and adult dogs. Senior dogs may not have the capability to learn an entirely new technique but are proven to respond well to other easier techniques like positive reinforcement. Pet clickers can be purchased at any local pet store in your neighborhood.

1. Start by testing out your clicker. There should be an obvious button for you to press. Once you hear a two-toned click noise means you have succeeded. This will be the sound that you use after your dog has completed an action. Follow up with a reward.
2. Press your clicker right after the desired behavior has been achieved. Timing is extremely important because if you are delayed, your dog won't be able to associate that action with the click. Reward your dog with a treat after the click. The timing of the treat is less important in this case.
3. You can use your clicker every time you see your dog doing something that is good. For example, if you see your dog beginning to sit on his/her own, you can use the clicker right away and then provide a reward.
4. If you are trying to express positive enthusiasm, don't increase the number of clicks but instead increase the number of rewards.

5. Keep training sessions short and sweet as dog learn more in multiple 5 minute sessions compared to 30 minute long sessions.

6. You can curb bad behavior by clicking more at good behavior. Give your dog a click when he/she is going to the bathroom outside, even if they already learned this behavior. By continuously to reinforce this behavior will lower the chances of your dog forgetting with old age.

7. You can click even if your dog does accidental movements towards the desired behavior. Don't physically help your dog into a position that you want but let your dog discover this behavior on his/her own and follow up with a click and reward.

8. Don't only click when your dog exhibits the behavior perfectly. You can click and reward for small movements in the right direction. For example, if you are commanding your dog to stay, you can start to click if he/she begins to get into a crouching position.

9. If/when your dog is more advanced with their good behavior, you can begin to raise your goal. For example, if your dog is sitting down, begin to ask him to sit for longer. Wait a few moments longer than you would normally click, then click and reward. This technique is called "shaping" and helps you fine-tune your dog's already learned behaviors.

10. Often times, your dog will learn that hearing a click means a reward. He/she may begin to show you good behavior randomly. This could be in the form of sitting whenever he/she sees you or lying down when he/she sees you. If you have reached this point, you can now introduce a cue. This can be in a hand signal, word, or both. If your dog succeeds at listening to the cue, you can reward. Always

ignore spontaneous learned behavior if you have not provided your dog with a cue.

The most important thing with this training is the timing of your clicks. Make sure you are not clicking too late as you may accidentally teach a different behavior to your dog. Be consistent and have fun with your dog! This is a great bonding experience.

Mirror Training

Mirror training is a type of training that is based on the research and theory that dogs learn through example. The idea behind this is that if your dog is provided with a model that has good behavior, your dog will rival against this dog in competition for rewards. Your dog will begin to copy and mimic behaviors to learn which ones are most desired. Often times, you can use a different dog as the model or a human can act as a model as well. You begin this training by letting your dog watch you interact with the model and praise them for good behavior while scolding the bad behaviors. Your dog as the observer will learn that certain behaviors warrant a reward while other behaviors don't.

This type of training is less popular because of the lower success rate. It also requires more resources, such as a model, and is often inconvenient for most dog trainers. It also needs to partner with the positive reinforcement technique to create successful results.

Scientific Training

Scientific training is a type of training that is mostly used by dog training professionals. This training relies completely on the newest information and research regarding dog behaviors. Since research is always discovering new things, this type of training is not as consistent and is always adapting. Since scientific dog training is extremely broad, it is impossible to pinpoint one specific method. Often times, scientific training is used with positive reinforcement training to have some sort of back bone structure. The mentality behind scientific training is that you shouldn't have to always rely on rewards to achieve a desired behavior. They believe that you can simply use a dog's psychology to improve the relationship between human and dog.

Relationship-Based Training

Relationship-Based Training is a technique that combines multiple training methods. Its main focus is to create a customized approach for a specific dog and human relationship. The theory behind this training is that the bond that a dog and a human share is the main driver of everything. This technique aims to help the dog achieve its needs in order to improve their overall communication. This technique revolves around being mutually beneficial.

In order for this type of training to be successful, the owner has to have a good understanding of their dog's body language. They must also know what rewards are the most motivating for their dog and how to achieve his/her needs. This type of training requires a lot of time and patience but creates a very deep bond between human and dog. There isn't a specific set of instructions for this like Clicker Training, but it solely relies on you being able to come to an understanding with your dog.

HOW TO CORRECT BEHAVIORAL PROBLEMS

CORRECTING behavioral problems is something that all dog owners need to prepare for, as this is an obstacle that every dog owner faces. Remember, it is easier to prevent behavioral problems than to correct them, but obviously, we can't prevent everything. So, arming yourself with the knowledge of how you can correct behavioral problems will help make your life a little bit easier. Behavioral problems can range from chewing up furniture, using the bathroom inside or constant barking. In this chapter, I will teach you various methods that you can follow to help correct behavioral problems and to reduce the chances of them arising.

Managing Your Dog's Energy

A common problem that dog owners struggle with is managing their dog's energy. You would be surprised at how few behavioral problems will arise as long as your dog's energy is well-managed. A healthy dog in adulthood needs a lot of exercise or entertainment if nobody is home. If someone is leaving their dog all day at home alone, you may soon realize that your dog may turn to destructive behavior to cure his/her boredom and to burn off some energy. Simply fix this problem by providing your dog with more outdoor exercise time. Bring your dog to the dog park every single day to run around with other dogs. If you are gone for 8 - 10 hours during the day, consider hiring a dog walker or someone to come and walk/exercise your dog. If your dog has extremely high energy levels, you may want to consider signing them up for agility training. If your dog's energy levels are managed properly, you will find that your dog has less bad behavior to exhibit.

Managing Your Dog's Impulses/Urges

If you have recently adopted an adult dog into your home, they may be more reactive to their emotions. They may be more prone to barking at any small noises or getting overly excited during human meal times. Often, dogs do unwanted behaviors due to pettiness or frustration. Try to pay a lot of attention to your dog and notice if he/she is trying to show you that they are frustrated. By training your dog the basic commands, you can help manage your dog's impulses by using a command such as "sit" or "stay" whenever they are acting out.

Teaching/Reinforcing Basics

Make sure your dog still has a good understanding of basic behavioral and house training. If your dog is heading towards an older age, he/she may have forgotten some of the stuff that he/she used to know. Make sure to always be reinforcing good behaviors every so often in order for your dog to remember which types of behaviors are good and which aren't. Most people tend to forget to reinforce basic things like using the bathroom outside or not jumping on people. Make sure you are intermittently rewarding your dog with treats or praise after they successfully greet someone or have used the bathroom outside. This will prevent future behavioral problems when your dog reaches seniorhood.

Rewarding Your Dog for Positive Behaviors

Positive reinforcement is extremely important when trying to teach your dog what behaviors are good and which aren't. Make sure to always ask yourself if you have reinforced good behavior recently. A tip here is to always have treats nearby that you can give to your dog when they exhibit behaviors that you want. If you haven't, your dog may be prone to forgetting good behaviors later on with old age. You can always reinforce by bringing reward back into you and your dog's life. It will be a nice surprise for your dog and good for their behavior in the future.

Properly Utilizing Negative Reinforcement

You should NEVER use harsh punishment with your dog as studies have shown that that is ineffective for dogs. Instead, negative reinforcement should always be in the form of no attention and no awards. If you catch your dog chewing up your favorite pair of shoes, simply take them away and don't give any more attention. Your dog will likely learn pretty quickly that that type of behavior does not get him/her any attention. Never use practices like smacking your dog as punishment as this just creates fear, not respect. This will likely cause your dog to do bad behaviors when you are not around. Instead, no matter how angry or upset you are, simply ignore your dog and move on. Continue to positively reinforce him/her when they are exhibiting good behavior.

Instilling Confidence In Your Dog

A confident dog is a happy dog. Dogs that are shy and fearful tend to exhibit more negative behaviors compared to dogs that are outgoing and confident. If you notice that your dog is exhibiting behavioral problems such as fear, shyness, or loneliness - it could be due to the lack of confidence. You can help your dog build more confidence by bringing him/her outside for more socialization. Take baby steps and start off with arranging one on one doggy play dates with another dog. Slowly work your way up to introducing your dog to the dog park, where they are able to interact with multiple dogs and people at the same time.

Building a Strong Bond With Your Dog

Enforcing a good relationship between you and your dog is extremely important, especially when they are in their adulthood or seniorhood. If you find that you haven't been having enough bonding time with your dog, try to schedule some quality time. Do activities like playing, brushing, grooming, and petting. These are all things that your dog will enjoy and will bring you guys even closer. Having a close bond with your dog will ensure that you understand a lot of your dog's body language and what they are trying to communicate to you. Knowing these things is extremely valuable as you can identify if something is wrong just by watching your dog's behavior.

Using Proper Technique During Training

If you are training an adult dog or senior dog, you have to make sure you are using good technique. Using techniques incorrectly can cause confusion with dogs, thus making training more difficult and tedious. Start from the basics and make sure you are consistent with the technique you are using. For example, if you are deciding to use clicker training with your dog, always have the clicker on you and always click before you present reward. Any inconsistencies will throw your dog off and make the training process more difficult.

TRAINING YOUR DOG FOR PUBLIC SITUATIONS

AT THIS POINT in the book, you should have a direction where you want to take the training for your dog. The next step is to properly train your dog for outside situations as you will likely be taking your dog for lots of walks and visits to the dog park. Training your dog for public situations is a combination of learning the right technique for walking your dog and obedience training. Obedience training is often utilized during these situations as your dog may get overly excited when they see other dogs or friendly people. You may need to use certain commands to control their behavior to prevent any accidents. Let's first take a look at how to properly walk your dog.

How to Walk Your Dog

One of the hardest parts about managing your dog's behavior outside of your home is while you are walking him/her on a leash. This takes up almost 99% of the time you are outside with your dog. Learning the proper walking techniques will make your life easier and your dog happier. Let's take a look at 10 different walking tips that you should follow to make the walks with your dog more enjoyable and manageable.

1. If your dog pulls on your leash, use a front clip harness.

Many dogs that are excited tend to constantly pull on their leashes. Certain dog collars and leashes actually make it easy for dogs to pull more and promotes more pulling during a walk. Getting a front clip harness is one of the best investments you can make when it comes to walking your dog. When you are shopping for this leash, check the front of the dog harness to see if there is a clip at the front of the harness. Although having a front clip harness won't solve all your problems, it certainly makes it harder for your dog to get into the habit of pulling.

2. Allow your dog to sniff his/her surroundings.

Although to you, walking your dog may be a necessity to let your dog relieve him/herself while giving him/her exercise. However, to your dog, the walks are the only time during the day that they can go out and explore. Give your dog some extra time and let them explore their surroundings and sniff around. This will help them get socialized better to the environment they're in. If you don't want to stop every 10 seconds to let your dog sniff around, choose areas that you deem are safe and appropriate and allow your dog to sniff around and explore. All the smells that your dog is experiencing provide them with information and stimulation. It is your dog's way to keep track of everything that's going on in your neighborhood. Also, sniffing takes energy; you'd be surprised at how much more energy is burned if you allow your dog to sniff his/her environment.

3. Don't use retractable leashes when walking your dog.

A rule of thumb for most experienced dog owners is to avoid using retractable leashes on walks. Retractable leashes cause numerous hazards compared to your traditional leashes. The problem with retractable leashes is that the length of the leash itself makes it hard for you to control your dog, especially if you are walking in busy areas. Most dogs can easily run into the street with retractable leashes as they are not easy to reel in. Those locks that are in retractable leashes have also been known to disengage if pulled on with enough pressure. Retractable leashes have also been known to injure both dogs and humans. The next time you go shopping for a new leash, avoid retractable leashes, and stick with front clip harnesses.

4. Always clean up after your dog.

When walking your dog, always remember to pick up your dog's poop. This simple action is much more than just being a good neighbor. Dog poop that is left in public causes many health concerns to both humans and dogs. Dog poop can contain dangerous organisms like E. coli and salmonella. This can easily be spread to other animals in your area. Make sure you are always stocked up on poop bags; they are cheap and can be bought in any pet store or even convenience store. Opt for the biodegradable ones if possible!

5. Bring plenty of water during your walks.

If it is summer or you are living in a warm climate, make sure you bring enough water for your dog. Dog's have difficulty regulating their temperature compared to humans. It is actually very easy for dogs to overheat. They can become dehydrated quite easily if they go without water for a while. Buy a collapsible water bottle and give your dog water every 30 minutes or so.

6. Make sure your dog has an ID tag.

Every time you and your dog leave your home, make sure they are wearing a form of identification. Accidents happen and dogs can accidentally run away from their owners during walks. In order to be able to track your dog down afterward, make sure they are microchipped so if anyone finds them, they can contact you through the information on the microchip. Having a dog tag with your dog's information and your contact information will ensure that whoever finds your dog can contact you in a timely manner.

7. Be careful of hot pavements during the summertime.

Depending on where you live, summers may get hot enough where the pavement can literally burn your skin. Before you take your dog out on a walk on pavement, place your hand on the ground to see how hot it is. Hold your hand there for at least 5 seconds; if the pavement feels too hot, then it is definitely too hot for your dog's paws. Instead, opt for a walk in the grass or in the woods. If your dog is tolerant of it, you can get your dog some booties/shoes to protect their paws.

8. Bring dog treats to keep your dog focused.

Every where that you go to walk, your dog will be filled with numerous distractions. Make sure you bring plenty of treats for you in order to practice some obedience training and positive rein-forcement when they complete a desired command or behavior. For instance, if your dog is distracted and wanting to chase after a squirrel, get his/her attention by telling her to sit/stay and provide him/her with a treat once it's achieved!

9. Ask owners before approaching their dog.

Although most dogs are pleasant around other dogs, this is not always 100% the case. Don't take any risks and ask the dog's owner that your dog wants to approach if they're okay with it. Most owners know whether their dog is good with other dogs or not. Check with them before allowing an interaction so no acci-dents happen!

10. Wear reflective gear if walking at night.

Just like your neighborhood runners, make sure you and your dog are wearing some sort of reflective gear if you're taking him/her out at night. Some nights can be extremely poor for visibility; don't take any risks and make sure that you are clearly visible by everyone else on the road.

Using Obedience Training During Walks

Obedience training is crucial when walking your dog in public. Simple commands such as "sit" and "stay" can change a situation dramatically. Make sure your dog has basic obedience training and is able to listen to commands outside of your home before taking him/her out for long walks or to dog parks. Let's do a quick review of what obedience training is.

The idea behind obedience training is to train your dog into 100% obedience using commands. This is a more advanced level of training, and your dog should already have basic knowledge of behavioral training. The main difference between behavioral training and obedience training is that you don't need a reason or specific behavior to initiate a command. For example, in behavioral training if your dog was jumping at a guest, you would use the command 'sit' to prevent that bad action. In obedience training, you are giving your dog commands regardless of the circumstance and they will listen to you 100%.

Most puppies or younger dogs will go through beginner level obedience training, which is simply by learning the common commands. Once your dog has the basics down, they should be able to learn more difficult and advanced level commands. Obedience training is required for your dog to participate in even more advanced levels of training such as agility training or vocational training. During obedience training, your dog will learn commands via verbal cues and non-verbal cues like hand gestures.

As we learned earlier, be sure to have trained your dog to be able to utilize these five commands when you are out in public:

- "Sit": Your dog will be in a sitting position where his/her front paws are in front of them, and their buttocks are touching the floor.
- "Down": Your dog is in a position where he/she is lying down. His/her front feet, legs, and chest are touching the ground.
- "Come": Your dog will come to you.
- "Stay": Your dog will stay still in the same position as to where you made that command.
- "Heel": Your dog's head will be parallel to your legs when you guys are walking. If he/she is in front of you, he/she will come back to your side.

TEACHING YOUR DOG COMMANDS

IN THE LAST chapter of this book, I want to teach you a little bit more regarding the different types of commands you can teach your dog. You have learned a few of the basic commands throughout this book, such as sit, stay, down, come and heel. However, there are so many more commands that your dog is capable of learning. I will be teaching you about some of these commands and how they can be used to benefit your overall relationship.

Advanced-Level Commands

In order to learn more advanced level commands, you will need to utilize various training methods like clicker training and positive reinforcement training. However, keep in mind that some of the more advanced level commands may require a professional trainer to help you with. Some of these require the trainer to have detailed knowledge of dog behavior and psychology. You can also utilize many YouTube videos where you can find examples of dog trainers utilizing various techniques to teach their dogs more advanced level commands. Take a look at the following list of advanced level commands that you can teach your dog:

- "Back Up"

This command will require your dog to step back a few steps from where they were standing. This command is useful for larger dogs that may be making other humans or dogs uncomfortable.

- "Leave it"

This command is used so your dog will not touch the object he/she is looking at. This is commonly used to get your dog to leave an item alone, like an accidentally dropped piece of food.

- "Get in" or "Go to bed"

This command will require your dog to go to their doggy bed and stay there until you give them the okay. This is different from 'stay' as your dog will have the freedom to move around within that location. This is really useful when you are trying to keep your dog away from a chaotic situation.

- "With me"

This command requires your dog to walk adjacent to you. This is similar to heel but your dog is not allowed to walk at a slower or faster pace than you. It is commonly used by owners to free-walk their dogs.

- "Stop"

This command will require your dog to stop whatever he/she is doing and get into the "down" position. This command should be effective no matter how far away you are from your dog.

- "Stand"

When you use this command, your dog will stand still. This is similar to 'stay,' but the difference is that your dog is standing. This is useful during grooming or teeth brushing.

- "Give"

This command requires your dog to give you an object that he/she is holding in their mouth. They will place the object into your hands. This is best used when playing fetch or if your dog has an object in his/her mouth.

- "Roll Over"

This command requires your dog to get into down position, roll over, then stand up. This is also just a fun trick that owners can teach their dogs.

- "Steady"

his command is used to help your dog walk freely without the use of a leash. When you use this command, your dog should close the distance between you and him/her and not dash away.

- "Place"

his command requires your dog to go to a specific place that you have previously set. Your dog will stay there until you give him/her the cue to come back. This is useful to keep your dog away from the door if you have people coming into your home. This is a more advanced version of getting your dog to 'sit' and 'stay.'

- "Shake"

his command will require your dog to shake his/her entire body. This is useful after bathing your dog or after a swim.

- "Drop" or "Drop it"

his command will require your dog to drop whatever is in his/her mouth. Dogs pick up random items all the time so this command is extremely useful if you catch them holding something that is unsafe. This is very useful to prevent them from eating dangerous things outside or destroying your belongings.

- "Speak"

*T*his command requires your dog to bark at your command. This normally used as a fun trick.

- "Take it"

*T*his command requires your dog to take the item you are holding out of your hand. Or, your dog will leave an item alone that you've commanded him/her to, but when you say 'take it,' that's their cue to grab it.

- "Growl"

*T*his command will require your dog to growl. This is normally commanded by the use of a subtle hand gesture rather than a vocal cue. This command is likely used by owners with special needs that want to warn others to stay away. The growl itself is not aggressive in nature but will be intimidating to others.

- "Fetch"

*T*his command requires your dog to retrieve a toy or an object that is thrown by someone. This is normally used during playtime and a good way to create an exercise for your dog.

- "Attack"

*T*his command requires your dog to attack something or someone. This is not recommended to be taught to a regular pet dog. This is normally used in guard dogs or police dogs.

*F*un Games to Help Learn Commands

Training your dog is serious business, but it doesn't always have to be! You can help your dog learn positive behaviors and new tricks through the use of games as well. Games are not only fun for both the human and the dog, but it is also useful in helping dogs manage energy and impulses. You can incorporate some training into these games by utilizing commands during them to ensure that your dog can still show obedience even when they are engaged during fun times. Let's take a look at a few games that I like to play with my dogs.

1. Frisbee

*F*risbee is a common and fun game that a lot of dog owners play with their dog. This is an advanced level of fetch as it encourages your dog to run long distances and to jump very high. Since dogs have the natural drive to chase and catch things, frisbee would be able to satisfy this natural instinct.

*I*ntroduce Frisbee to your dog by using a soft disc. Since traditional frisbees are very hard, your dog may injure him/herself and could discourage him/her from playing. Start with baby steps and throw the frisbee at short distances and let your dog catch it easily. Start to increase the difficulty as they get better by throwing it over further distances and higher off the ground as well. You can take a game of frisbee one level higher by playing with other dogs as well. This will create some healthy competition and result in more exercise for your dog and other dogs.

1. Flirt Poles

A lot of the times, when you see a flirt pole you think of cats. However, they are extremely useful in stimulating your dog physically and mentally. They are extremely effective for dogs that have high energy levels as one quick session can tire out a dog. A flirt pole is a long pole that has a rope attached to the end of it. At the end of the rope there is a lure that is used to entice your dog. They are great in terms of enticing your dog to do a lot of exercise and you can also practice some impulse control by telling your dog to let go of the pole on command.

W hen you are playing with your dog using the flirt pole, be sure to let your dog 'win' or catch the lure occasionally as a reward. This will make the game more fun for them and encourage them to keep playing in the future. If they never get to win, they will likely become disinterested in the game. Take it easy when you are first starting this game with your dog. This is a very high impact game and can be rough on your dog's joints, so avoid doing this if your dog is in their seniorhood.

1. Mini agility courses

*W*e talked a lot about agility training throughout this book, and a DIY agility course is a great way to introduce your dog to it. Agility courses are a great way for your dog to learn some new tricks and also a great mental work out as well.

*Y*ou can build one quite easily by purchasing some pylons that you can teach your dog to run around. You can slowly make it more difficult by building a DIY jump or DIY crawl tunnels. You can go an even more, simpler route and just purchase a hula hoop for your dog to jump through. Start off by holding the hula hoop just above the ground and slowly increase the height as your dog gets the hang of it. Begin to incorporate more and more into your obstacle course as your dog starts to get the hang of it.

1. Water games

*I*n the summertime, these are some of the most fun games you can play with your dog. If your dog already knows how to swim, bring along some toys to the pool or the beach and play a game of fetch in the water. Make sure your toys are able to float, so you don't lose them. If your dog doesn't know how to swim, you can purchase a doggie life jacket that will help them float.

· · ·

*I*f your dog isn't a great swimmer or is not that comfortable in the water, you can play some water games in your backyard. You can either set up a kiddy pool with shallow water where your dog can play in, or you can use a simple garden hose to entertain your dog. All you have to do is start spraying the house and let your dog run through it and around it.

1. Kong toys

*K*ong toys are one of the easiest games to play with your dog that requires minimal work. You can simply purchase a Kong toy at any pet store and place your dog's favorite treats on the inside. This game helps stimulate a dog's natural scavenging ability and can keep them entertained for hours.

*Y*ou can choose to stuff your Kong toy with healthy treats or a mix of a few different things. Some people like to freeze the kong toy with some treats and chicken broth in it. This way will increase the difficulty of your dog getting access to the treats as he/she would have to get through all the broth first. This toy works wonders to keep your dog entertained while you are away. You can get into the habit of giving your dog the Kong toy before you leave for your day. This way, your dog will be less anxious about you leaving and more focused on the excitement of that toy.

1. Kiss

*Y*ou can teach your dog a cool trick like how to kiss your cheek! This is an extremely fun party trick and will 100% impress all your family and friends. Teaching your dog how to kiss is usually taught through the use of clicker training. First, get a sticky note and stick it to your hand. Then, get your dog to sniff the sticky note, and every time he/she successfully sniffs it you reward with a treat. Do this until your dog sniffs the sticky note 100% of the time. Now, it's time to add a cue. Move the sticky note further away and at a higher angle and say "kiss." Once your dog sniffs the sticky note, click, and reward. Keep doing this while using the cue until your dog completes it 100% of the time. Then, you will place the sticky note on your cheek and say "kiss!". If your dog successfully sniffs the sticky note on your cheek, click, and reward. Then, once your dog successfully is able to sniff the sticky note on your face 100% of the time, you can remove the sticky note. Finally, tell your dog to "kiss!" and if he/she is able to kiss your cheek without the sticky note, click, and reward. Voila! You have now taught your dog how to kiss you!

CONCLUSION

There are definitely numerous topics you need to take into consideration when it comes to training your dog. Regardless of what type of training you decide to do with your dog, the most important part is reinforcement. Without reinforcement, your dog may forget what he/she has learned very quickly. The age of your dog also plays a huge role in this as puppies tend to forget training quicker than older dogs. However, they absorb new information very fast; you just have to remember to keep reinforcing it to prevent forgetfulness.

Adult dog and senior dogs are generally more emotionally mature and can learn just as well as puppies. Although it's true that puppies learn faster, older dogs can learn new tricks as well. Throughout this book, you learned multiple ways to tackle training based on your specific dog. You've learned that different breeds (big vs. small), age, size of your home, and your personal lifestyle plays a huge role in what type of training will be most efficient and appropriate. By making sure your dog is well trained to the specificity of your needs, you will ensure that your companionship with your dog is fulfilling, loving, and mutually beneficial.

To end off this book, I want to make sure you leave with an understanding that choosing the right type of training for your dog based on their age, breed, and your lifestyle is crucial. If you are still unsure, revisit earlier chapters where I have outlined for you how these factors affect the training of your dog. Keep in mind that you should ALWAYS be reinforcing positive behaviors in your dog even if your dog hasn't forgotten them. It is always better to prevent behavioral problems than to try to correct them later. Be sure to also be looking out for your dog's behaviors as certain things they do can indicate health issues or underlying issues. Catching these types of problems early on will allow you to fix them before anything gets serious. Catching certain health issues late may increase the risk of your dog not being able to make it or causing an extremely expensive vet bill. This is also why taking your dog to the vet frequently is important as your vet can give you frequent updates on your dog's health and advise you if anything needs to be adjusted or changed.

So what's next for you and your dog? Depending on your needs, you may want to take your dog training to the next level and learn more advanced-level commands and tricks. Or, you can simply continue reinforcing existing good behaviors and commands. Your relationship with your dog should be one of harmony. Properly caring for your dog while teaching him/her the necessary behaviors and commands is your one way ticket to having a successful relationship with him/her. To you, your dog is a part of your world but to your dog, you are their entire world. You mean everything to them, and you are the person that they look forward to seeing the most. Do your absolute best when it comes to building a relationship with him/her and be sure to always be taking care of your dog. Things like bathing, dental care and socialization are all important aspects of a dog's training that will ultimately impact their general behavior. By always making sure you are taking care of these things, you are lowering the chances of your dog exhibiting bad behavior due to unmet needs. It will also help you prevent expensive trips to the vet for issues like teeth rot or skin problems. Pay attention to your dog's caretaking needs and I promise the favor will be returned.